Mini-Lathe Magic
Big Projects From A Small Lathe

Ron Hampton

Schiffer Publishing Ltd

4880 Lower Valley Road, Atglen, PA 19310 USA

Dedication

To Barbara—my wife, best friend, and companion. Thank you! You can never know how much your love and support mean to me. And thanks for tolerating my "dusty" hobby.

Acknowledgments

I would like to thank the following people for their help: Les Stevenson, for loaning me his Delta Midi lathe and Buddy Rose, for making me the tool holder that fits onto my lathe. I appreciate Robert Rosand, Kelly Dunn, and Max Krimmel, who sent me photographs to put into the Gallery. Additionally, I want to thank Woodcraft Supply of Dallas (1-800-535-4486), who gave me a tool rest when mine broke. I also want to thank Steve, of The Cutting Edge of Houston (1-800-790-7980), for getting me some supplies in a hurry when I needed them. I also want to thank Craft Supplies (1-800-551-8876).

Contents

Copyright © 2002 by Ron Hampton
Library of Congress Control Number: 2002108481

ISBN: 0-7643-1614-1
Printed in China

All photographs taken by Ron Hampton, with the exception of those provided by the professional turners for the gallery.

Published by Schiffer Publishing Ltd.
4880 Lower Valley Road
Atglen, PA 19310
Phone: (610) 593-1777; Fax: (610) 593-2002
E-mail: Schifferbk@aol.com
Please visit our web site catalog at **www.schifferbooks.com**
We are always looking for people to write books on new and related subjects. If you have an idea for a book please contact us at the above address.

This book may be purchased from the publisher.
Include $3.95 for shipping.
Please try your bookstore first.
You may write for a free catalog.

In Europe, Schiffer books are distributed by
Bushwood Books
6 Marksbury Ave.
Kew Gardens
Surrey TW9 4JF England
Phone: 44 (0)20-8392-8585
Fax: 44 (0)20-8392-9876
E-mail: Bushwd@aol.com
Free postage in the UK. Europe: air mail at cost

Introduction

Woodturning is experiencing tremendous growth in popularity around the world. Many people are finding that they now have the time and money to be able to enjoy new hobbies. Others find that they would like to slowly move into a new career direction. Woodturning is the perfect answer for many people. It is a wonderfully satisfying hobby and can be a terrific source of additional income. For the hobbyist, woodturning can be richly rewarding as a means of artistic expression and as a means of relaxation. For the professional, woodturning can be a pleasant lifestyle that gives the turner a desirable form of employment.

The recent advent of the "Midi" or "Mini" lathe has created quite a revolution in turning. When I got started in turning about eight years ago, it was necessary to have a heavy expensive lathe if you wanted a good lathe. The idea that a small inexpensive lathe could be a good lathe was ridiculous. The introduction of the Jet "Mini"™ lathe and, more recently, the Delta "Midi"™ have shown that high quality lathes can be small and inexpensive.

I demonstrated at the 2000 American Association Of Woodturners National symposium in Charlotte, North Carolina, using the Jet Mini-lathe. For most woodturners, demonstrating at the national meeting is one of our ultimate goals. I had my choice of any lathe made, but for my demonstration the Jet "Mini" lathe was the best lathe. It was my first choice!

Now that you have a terrific new Mini or Midi lathe, you need to learn how to use it!! Terrific!! This book is going to get you well started on your new turning adventure. You will have a lot of fun learning to use your lathe if you will spend a few minutes learning how to use it safely.

ALL wood working equipment can be dangerous if used improperly. The wood lathe is no different. The Mini-lathe can be dangerous if you do not use proper technique or if you ignore correct turning procedures. But, turning can be very safe and a tremendous amount of fun if you follow the safety instructions provided both by the manufacturer of your lathe and in this book, and the safety guidelines of the AAW.

I will do everything that I can in these sixty-four pages to teach you how to be a terrific turner. But, there are other ways to increase your turning skills. You can learn from tapes, books, live demonstrations, and hands on experience. I have benefited from all of the above. Remember that learning takes time, patience, and practice. You do not learn to turn just by watching somebody. You must do it! So, try to practice some of the following turning techniques almost every day for a few minutes. If you do so, you will quickly see improvement in your skill level.

In the section "A Few Good Tools" I will go over a short list of tools that I think you need to get started. Try to resist the urge to go out and purchase a large selection of tools. I did that and most of my expensive collection hangs on a wall and is never used.

One of the most important lessons that you will soon learn is that dull tools do not cut. With that important message out of the way, we will teach you how to quickly sharpen your tools to get good results.

We will also cover nine terrific projects that will get you well into the turning game. By the time you have done each of these projects several times you will have acquired considerable turning skill. Have fun and continue to learn. There is a whole world of possibilities in turning, and a lifetime of fun.

Lathe Safety

Working with the lathe can be a lot of fun and it can be very safe if you follow the safety rules and pay attention. However, any and all equipment and hand tools can be dangerous!! So, to have fun and be safe at the same time it is necessary to follow some basic safety rules and understand why there are rules.

1. **Speed kills!** That is true about drugs, cars, **and machinery**. You are turning an object with a lathe. If the object gets away from you or comes apart, then it can become a lethal flying object. That is why, in this book, we have the speed set at the lowest speed possible, 500RPM. All projects are done at the lowest speed. We are doing big projects compared to the size of the lathe and it is necessary to go slow. The only places in the book where we go to a faster RPM are in the next two sections—Turning Tools, where we are learning to use the tools, and Sharpening Tools—and in the final chapter, where we will be making some very small turnings. In those cases we will be turning at 1000 RPM.

2. **Sober and alert!** When working in the shop you must always be sober and alert. If you are too tired or in too big of a hurry to do something the correct way, then it is time for you to quit and go to the house. You cannot do good work if you are compromised. Remember, it is very easy to get hurt.

3. **Safety equipment:** Always wear the proper safety equipment. This means that you always put a face shield on before turning on the lathe. **Always!!!** Anytime you are making any dust, you must have a respirator or air filter on. If you are too tired to wear the filter, then you are too tired to work. That is OK. Quit and go to the house. The more comfortable your safety equipment is, the more likely you are to use it. So shop around and get the best, most comfortable safety equipment you can find. (Notice I did not say the cheapest equipment you can find.) Safety equipment includes but is not limited to the following:

1. A sturdy face shield.
2. Air filter or respirator.
3. Shop apron with no lose sleeves or strings to get caught.
4. Plastic safety glasses.
5. No loose jewelry (watches, chains, rings), hair, or clothing.

I will briefly talk about each one of the above.

A sturdy face shield is necessary because wood comes apart and it comes off the lathe. Every woodturner can tell you stories of being hit by their turning.

The air filter is necessary to protect you from dust and fumes from finishing agents. We can be allergic to the dust or we can become infected by the fungus that is in spalted wood.

Spalted wood is wood that is partially decayed by fungus. The fungus may cause attractive patterns or color in wood. Highly figured or colored spalted wood is very attractive and makes beautiful turnings. You must be very careful not to breathe the dust from spalted wood because this can lead to a lung fungus infection. If you decide to turn spalted wood, you must have very good systems in place to protect you from the dust. These systems include: good vacuum system, good air filtration, and a good respirator.

I had a friend who almost died from a lung infection caused by spalted wood. After a while I told my friend that he had "tortured" the physician enough and that he should tell the physician that he had been working with spalted wood. My friend informed the physician. The physician changed the medicine and my friend got well.

A shop apron gives you some protection and keeps a lot of dust off of you. Make sure that there are no loose ends in the front that can get caught in the spinning equipment. If you ever look at my homemade apron, you will be tempted to say "boy that is old and beat up." That is true. It has caught on fire three times while I made tools for my shop. It has also stopped flying objects and cyano-acrylic glue. One night, recently, it caught a piece of alabaster stone that I was turning. Is it beat up and rough looking? Yes. Am I going to get rid of it anytime soon? Not likely.

Plastic safety glasses are necessary if you wear glasses. Turning accidents are going to happen. We just need to make sure that you do not get hurt when it does occur.

No loose clothing, hair, or jewelry: Anything that can get caught will eventually get caught in a spinning lathe. No long hair, long sleeves, or jewelry. I no longer wear a watch or any rings. I just do not want them snatched off of me, taking a finger or hand with them. I had a friend one time get his tee shirt caught in a slow moving metal lathe while we made a part. He was slowly being pulled into the lathe. The two of us were able to stop the one horsepower motor until I was able to figure out how to reverse the motor. (I was not familiar with his lathe.) It was a tense couple of seconds. We would never be able to stop my three horsepower motor.

4. Nothing in the Line of Fire: With your tool rest in place between you and the turning, any flying object will almost always travel in a straight line away from the lathe or straight up. Make sure that your friends or dog are not in the line of fire. Before I moved to my metal shop, I killed windows in my garage on two different occasions. (I know much more about speed control now. I also know how to fix windows.)

5. No Unattended Machines: If you leave the machine, turn it off. Never walk away from a running lathe. And never walk across the path of a running lathe. Do not let a friend watch in the line of fire.

Turning Tools: A Basic Tool Set

The woodturner needs a basic set of tools to turn wood. The set should include: a 1/2-inch bowl gouge, a 1 inch skew, a thin parting tool, 1/2- to 1/4-inch round nose scraper, and a narrow tool rest. (See Figure 1.)

Later you might want to add a few other tools like: a 1/4-inch bowl gouge, 1/2-inch skew, additional scrapers, 4-jaw woodturning chuck, and an additional tool rest. (See Figure 2.)

The first tool to buy is a good 1/2-inch bowl gouge. Along with the gouge, purchase a David Ellsworth™ sharpening jig. (See Figure 3.) This jig allows you to put a super edge on your bowl gouge easily. And, just as important, you can quickly re-sharpen your bowl gouge. At my last woodturning meeting I had the members time me from the moment I left my lathe to the second I returned to the lathe. I walked to my sharpener, turned on the grinder, put the jig on my bowl gouge, sharpened the gouge, returned the jig to its home, turned off the grinder, and walked back to my lathe in 24.47 seconds. This is not enough time to keep you from having sharp tools.

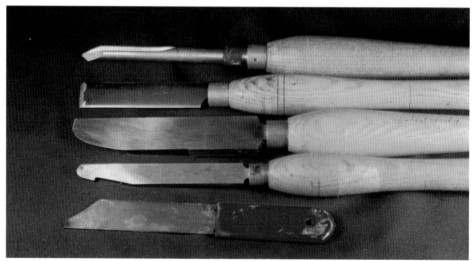

Figure 1. A basic set of tools to turn wood. The set should include: a 1/2-inch bowl gouge, a 1-inch skew, 1/2 to 1/4-inch round nose scraper, a thin parting tool, and a narrow tool rest.

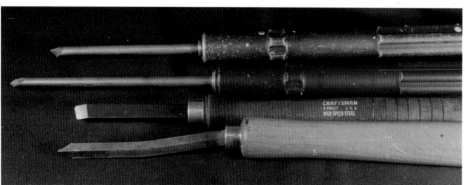

Figure 2. Later you might want to add a few other tools like (top to bottom): 1/4-inch bowl gouge, 1/2-inch skew, additional scrapers, a 4-jaw woodturning chuck, and additional tool rest. The chuck and the tool rest are not pictured here.

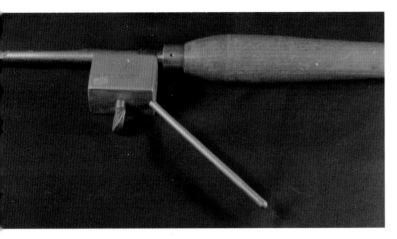

Figure 3. The first tool to buy is a good 1/2-inch bowl gouge. Purchase the David Ellsworth™ sharpening jig along with it. This jig allows you to put a super edge on your bowl gouge easily.

The second tool that you should get is a good scraper. I make a lot of my scrapers, but for this book I used two store bought scrapers. I used a 1-inch round scraper and a 1/4-inch round nose scraper. (See Figure 4.) I could have easily gotten by with the small scrapper.

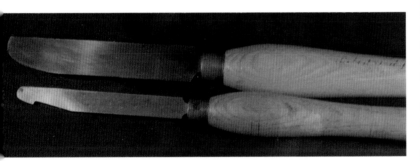

Figure 4. The second tool that you should get is a good scraper. I used a 1-inch round scraper and a 1/4-inch round nose scraper.

The third tool for your set is the skew. Getting the full use out of your skew requires quite a bit of practice. But you can do a lot of simple, but effective, scraping cuts with the skew right from the beginning. The standard skew is 1 1/4-inches wide with a straight edge that slopes. Later you may find that a 1/2-inch wide skew is handy.

The fourth tool is the thin parting tool. I like the Chris Scott™ thin parting tool. (See Figure 5.) I lost mine for a while and had to use some homemade thin parting tools for a while. They worked well but did not have the pretty red handle of the Chris Scott tool. (Okay, so I am a creature of habit, and I like the look and feel of the tool and do not want to change.) This tool allows you to make a thin parting cut that saves a lot of wood. This seemed to be necessary for me all the time. I guess I try to get too much from a piece of wood.

Figure 5. I like the Chris Scott™ thin parting tool. It saves a lot of wood by being thin and strong.

Learning to Use the Tools

Practice, practice, practice!!! Sorry, but you got to put the time in. There are ways to shorten the practice time in the process of mastering the tools. First, watch a good turner using his tools. There are a lot of good woodturning videos that show you how to use the tools. Study them. Then go practice.

Practice on cheap wood. Scrap pine 2x4's are good practice material. They are cheap or free. The wood is soft and hard to make clean cuts on. So when you start getting clean cuts on soft pine 2x4's, you have started to develop quite of bit of skill with the tool.

Cut the 2x4 into square 2x2 blanks about 6 to 8 inches long. Mount them between centers. (See Figure 6.) Make sure the tailstock is securely tightened and locked. Position the tool rest and check to make sure that the piece rotates freely without hitting the tool rest. Set the speed for about 750 or 1000 RPM. Put your face shield on. Stand to the side of the lathe as you turn on the lathe.

The Bowl Gouge

Sharpen your bowl gouge; then start making practice cuts. First start by making your turning blank round. Point the bowl gouge straight into the blank. Let it just barely touch the revolving 2x2. It will make a "click, click, click" as the bowl gouge cuts a corner of wood four times each time the wood makes a revolution. (See Figure 6.) Do this all along the length of the 2x2. Adjust your tool rest as necessary. This is called a "roughing out" cut.

Once the 2x2 starts becoming round, you can practice making a shear cut with the side of the tool. Adjust the tool rest close to the cylinder. Turn the bowl gouge sideways so that you can present the side of the bowl gouge to the cylinder. Allow the side of the gouge to make a thin slicing cut. (See Figure 7.) This is called a "finish cut." Practice making cove cuts with your bowl gouge. (See Figure 8.)

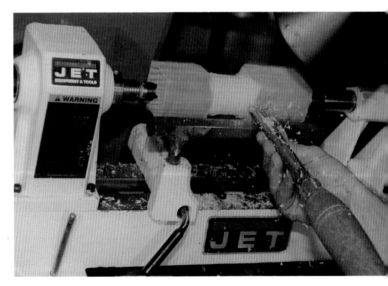

Figure 6. For practice, mount a 2x2 between centers. Make practice cuts to improve your skill.

Figure 7. Practice making a "finish cut" by allowing the side of the gouge to make a thin slicing cut.

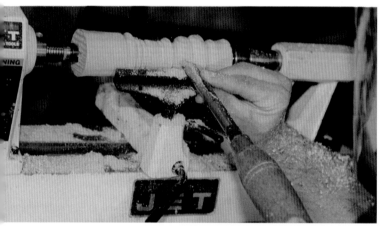

Figure 8. With a little practice you can make nice beads and coves with your bowl gouge.

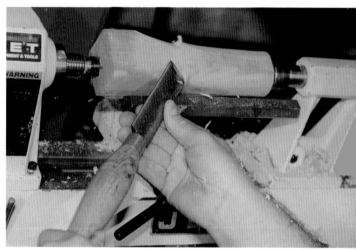

Figure 9. Practice with your skew. Start off by turning a square 2x2 round. This is a great learning experience.

Figure 10. Practice making beads on the smooth round cylinder. First mark off 1-inch sections. Then make a straight in cut with the skew.

The Skew

Mount a 2x2 the same way you did for the bowl gouge. Hold the skew at an angle so that it can make a slice at the edge of the wood. Barely allow it to touch the turning 2x2. Slowly advance from the middle of the turning toward the tailstock. (See Figure 9). Practice the same movement in the opposite direction. Do this until the 2x2 is round and smooth.

Practice making beads on the smooth round cylinder. First mark off 1-inch sections. Then make a straight in cut with the skew. (See Figure 10.) Then use the tip of the skew held at an angle to make a round slicing cut. (See Figures 11 and 12.) The first cut must be very small. On the next cut, go a little further away and do the same cut again. Each time you will make the cut a little bigger and deeper. This is a complex cut. The backhand starts out low and during the cut comes up so that it is level with the tool rest. Also, the skew is tilted away from the center and rotates to straight up and down during the cut. Once you master the cut you can get very smooth results. (See Figure 13.)

The Scraper

The scraper is probably the easiest tool to learn how to use. However, there are a few rules to its use. First, like all other tools it must be sharp. Second, for most cuts the scraper should be at or slightly above centerline. In this way, if you get a catch, the scraper will be thrown down into air and not destroy the turning. (This is a

Figure 11. Use the tip of the skew held at an angle to make a round slicing cut. The first cut must be very small

Figure 12. On the next cut with the skew, go a little further away from the deepest part of the cut and do the same cut again as in Figure 11.

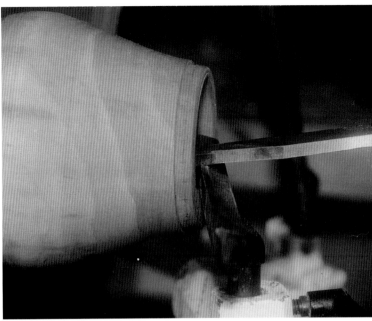

Figure 14. To remove the nub at the bottom of the bowl, position the scrapper below the nub.

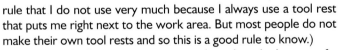

Figure 13. Once you master the cut you can get very smooth results. The pencil is pointing to the smooth cut on soft pine. You could start sanding this cut with 400 grit sandpaper.

rule that I do not use very much because I always use a tool rest that puts me right next to the work area. But most people do not make their own tool rests and so this is a good rule to know.)

The third rule concerns removing the nub at the bottom of a bowl. Position the scraper below the nub with the handle above the tip. (See Figures 14 and 15.) Lower the handle slowly. This will cause the cutting edge of the scraper to rise into the nub. This slow scraping motion will slowly cut the nub away. This means that the tool rest must be slightly above the nub.

Gentle scraping with a sharp tool can give a very nice cut. Very often this cut is the final cut for the inside of a bowl or box. Some turners use a scraper to get a very nice finish cut on the outside of a bowl. (I prefer a skew or bowl gouge, but it is just personal preference.)

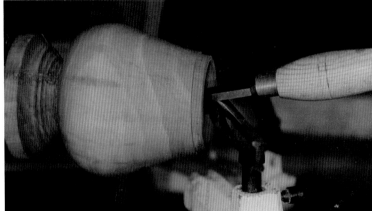

Figure 15. With the lathe running slowly, lower the handle so that the scrapper slowly comes up into the nub. This will slowly cut away the nub.

The Parting Tool

Most beginner tool sets come with a 1/4-inch wide parting tool. This will do for starting out. But you will eventually want to get a thin parting tool. Set your tool rest so that the cutting edge of the parting tool is at the centerline of the turning. Advance the tool in slowly. After making a little penetration into the wood, come out and widen the hole twice as wide as the cutting tool. This will give the shavings a place to exit and keep your tool from overheating. Hold the parting tool in a firm grip. If you make too deep a cut before you widen the cut, it is very easy for the parting tool to get flipped out of your hand, and come back and smash your finger. (I know that this scenario is hard to picture, but it is easy to do. Believe me. I have done it enough times.)

There are several dangers if you do not widen the hole as you cut in. First, the tool will heat up and get lodged in the cut. Then you can have a big accident as the tool gets flipped out of your hand. The second danger is that the tool heats up enough to burn the bottom of the turning. It is difficult to sand out a burned area and will require a considerable amount of time.

A Note About Homemade Tools

I make a lot of my own tools. I like to make tools. It is fun and allows me to have the specific tool I want without buying a tool and waiting for it to get here.

My opinion on tool steel is very different than the opinion of many turners of the world. My tool steel is whatever I have that is handy. My scrapers do not require High Speed Steel. It is true that cold roll steel tools do not hold an edge as long as HSS. But most beginning turners need the experience of learning how to sharpen their scrapers. So it is okay if you have to re-sharpen your tool every few minutes.

DO NOT USE A STEEL FILE FOR TOOL STEEL!!!!! The steel in a file has been hardened so that it will cut steel. This steel is very hard and very brittle. It is dangerous to a woodturner. A tool made from an old file could fracture with very sharp and dangerous edges. **If it fractured it could cut you severely and cause the loss of an eye.** The only way that "Bastard Steel" can be used is if it is heat-treated to make it softer by tempering. I can do this, but it is not a project for beginners.

Stay away from using files to make scrappers unless you are an experienced black smith!!!!! Even then, if I make a tool from a file, I make two at one time. I coat one in duct tape and put it in a vice. I put on a safety shield and very thick, heavy leather gloves. I then hit it with a big hammer. If it bends 90 degrees without breaking, then it passes the test. I throw that tool away and use the other one.

The Tool-Rest

The tool rest is a very important part of the lathe. In my opinion it is not given enough importance from the manufacturer of equipment. The tool rest must be able to reach many different areas. To cut well, your tool rest must be close to the wood. This means that several different shaped tool rests are necessary.

Factory Made Tool Rests

Most tool-rests from the factory are made from cast iron. To be strong, the cast iron needs to be thick and wide. This is hard, brittle metal. Hard, brittle metal is very dangerous to the woodturner because it can break.

Non-Breakable Steel

Tool rests should be made from cold-rolled steel. This steel can be bent, but it will not break. You might be able to break the weld, but the steel itself will not break. I make my tool rests from cold rolled steel. So far I have never had one break. You can have your local machine shop make you a tool rest from cold rolled steel. If you do not want to make your own tool rest, I make and sell tool rests. I may be contacted at:

Ron Hampton
4306 Texas Blvd.
Texarkana, TX 75503
www.woodturningplus.com
or 903-794-5386

A Near Accident

About two years after I started turning, I bought an old, used Powermatic lathe. It had a cast iron tool-rest. I got a bad catch that slapped my tool hard against the tool-rest. The cast iron tool rest broke, leaving a very sharp ragged edge. The force of the tool catch shoved my hand down against and past the sharp edges of the broken tool rest. The force of the accident, combined with the sharp edges, could have cut my fingers off.

I was wearing a leather glove with the fingertips cut out. This gave me quite a bit of protection. However, the force of the accident pushed my fingers down past the rugged edge of the broken tool rest. The broken tool rest was very sharp and ragged!! **It could have easily cut a finger off!!!**

I counted my fingers five times!!! After the fifth count I started to believe that I still had all of my fingers. **I had been very lucky!** The only time I have used a cast iron tool rest since then is when I was trying out my new mini lathe. The tool rest broke after very little use. **I checked to see if I was bleeding.** I was not. So I went over to my welding table and made an unbreakable steel tool rest. I pretty much will not use a cast iron tool rest any more.

An Unbreakable Tool Rest

From that time on, I started making all of my own tool rests. I use cold rolled steel. It can be bent, but it will not break!! The only place that could (in theory) break is the weld between the upright and the cross bar. I have never had one break. If it did break at that point, there would be no danger to the turner.

I make a tool rest to take care of any turning problem that I have. I have gotten used to having the correct tool rest for whatever turning problem that I have. It is nice!!

Specially Made Tool Rests for Mini (Midi) Lathes

I custom make five different tool rests for the mini (midi) lathe:

1. The standard tool rest is pictured on the far right in Figure 16. This can be made from channel steel to have a flat surface or made from round steel. Both are strong. It is designed to replace the tool rest that comes with your lathe.

2. The "Lazy J" tool rest is a bowl tool rest. It has two different curves that will snug up against almost any bowl that you will turn on your mini (midi) lathe. The "Lazy J" refers to the two different curves in the tool rest.

3. The tool rest on the far left of Figure 16 is called the "The Big Offset." It is made from 1-inch diameter steel and is

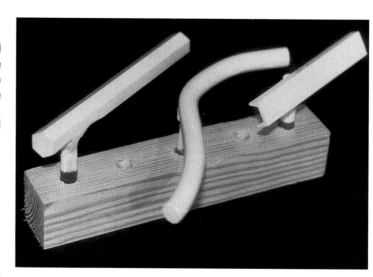

Figure 16. The standard tool rest is pictured on the far right in this photograph. The middle tool rest, the "Lazy J," is a bowl tool rest. It has two different curves that will snug up against almost any bowl that you will turn on your mini (midi) lathe. The tool rest on the far left is called the "The Big Offset."

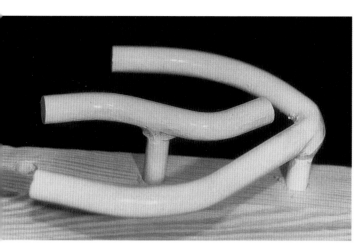

Figure 17. The tool rest on the left is called "The Small S" tool rest. It is terrific for many of the small turnings that you do on a small lathe. The tool rest on the right is called the "Wishbone Tool Rest." There will be many times that you will wish you had this tool rest!

6- to 8-inches long. This is the real workhorse of tool rests. The long side will reach most areas, and the short side will reach difficult spots. The entire length can be used to turn a long piece round. The large offset tool rest is designed to allow many of the steps in making a large bowl.

4. The tool rest on the left in Figure 17 is called "The Small S" tool rest. It is terrific for many of the small turnings that you do on a small lathe.

5. The tool rest on the right of Figure 17 is called "The Wishbone" tool rest. It is called this for two reasons. First, it is in the shape of a wishbone. This allows you to go abound the inside curve of a bowl easily. The other side allows you to cut the inside of the bowl easily. So easily, in fact, that you will wish that you had one like it. (Which is reason number two.)

These tool rests cost from $60 to $120 each. This may seem like a lot of money, but it is much cheaper than going to the emergency room to have a finger sewn back on. Besides that, it is fun to have the best tool to take care of a problem! If you are interested in having me make you one or more of these tool rests, you can contact me at:

Ron Hampton
4306 Texas Blvd
Texarkana, TX 75503
903-794-5386
Email: www.woodturningplus.com

Sharpening Tools

Being able to sharpen your tools quickly and easily is one of the most important skills a new turner must develop. Until recently most of the turning instructors felt that jigs were not worth having. They felt that you should spend years learning how to sharpen your tools, just like they did.

Fortunately, that outdated belief is dying. And I am proud to say that I have done my part to kill it. I do not drive a horse and buggy and I am not going to be forced to, just because my grandpappy did.

You can easily sharpen every woodturning tool you have with a very simple set up. You do not need to do as I did and buy every expensive sharpening system that is made. I presently use two different grinders, but that could be simplified to one grinder and do the same thing.

You need three basic components to your sharpening system. First you need a mid-sized grinder that runs at 1700 RPM. My Sears grinder with stand cost about $140 and is quite adequate. You can get bench top grinders for about $70. The grinder comes with a medium and a course grinding wheel. Replace the course wheel with a second medium wheel, so that both wheels are medium grit. The adjustable tool support on most grinders is inadequate. Be prepared to make or buy a more stable sharpening platform.

One wheel will be set up to sharpen scrapers. The other wheel will be set up to sharpen bowl gouges. Once set up, the arrangement should not be changed unless you decide you do not like that edge anymore and you are going to make a permanent change in the cutting edge of your tools.

Scrapers

Set the sharpening platform close to the grinding wheel and set the angle to 45 degrees from horizontal. (See Figure 18.) This is a Tobias Kaye sharpening system, which is very nice. This table is not adjustable, but I like the angle. On other platforms you can change the angle if you do not like it; however, I find this is a good angle for me. Once you find the correct angle, never reset the table. Every one of your scrapers will be sharpened to this angle. Every one will be perfectly sharp and every one will cut the same every day. This is a tremendous learning advantage. You will not have to be constantly learning how this "scraper" is cutting today.

Putting An Edge On Our Scrappers

Putting an initial edge on a scrapper may take several minutes. Your tools almost never arrive sharp from the factory. Most good factory made tools are made from high-speed steel (HSS). Present the metal to the wheel and slowly cut the metal. Rotate the tool so that you are sharpening all parts of the edge at approximately the same time. Do not overheat the metal. Stop to cool the metal often. Cool the metal by dipping it in water. Any metal may be burned, even High Speed Steel. Eventually the top edge of the tool will come in contact with the stone and a small spark will fly over the top of the tool. This part of the tool is now sharp. Rotate the tool so that a faint spark comes over all parts of the cutting edge. (See Figure 18.)

Figure 18. For scrapers set the sharpening platform close to the grinding wheel and set the angle to 45 degrees from horizontal.

Rub your finger or drag your thumbnail over this edge. You should have the same ground edge all the way around the scraper. (See Figure 19.) It should drag when pulled against your fingernail. Get used to checking your edge. You will soon learn the feel of a sharp tool. Remember to stop often from your turning to re-sharpen your tool.

Figure 19. Every one of your scrapers will be sharpened to this angle and every scraper will be perfect, every time. You can hone this edge with a diamond or with 400 grit sandpaper.

Re-Sharpening Your Scraper

Putting the correct initial edge on your scraper will take several minutes because you must keep the tool cool. However, re-sharpening the tool takes only a few seconds. My grinder takes a couple of seconds to come up to speed and it usually takes me about ten more seconds to re-sharpen my scraper. All I want is for just a hint of a spark to come over the scraper's entire cutting surface. I sharpen a scraper so quickly that most new woodturners think that I am pulling their leg. But that few seconds is all that it takes.

Honing

Occasionally I do an inside cut that must be very fine to make a very smooth cut. In this situation I will re-sharpen the scraper as I just described. Then I would hone the flat part of the scraper. To do this lay the hone on the flat part of the scraper and lightly rub back and forth. You are taking off the large bur and replacing it with a small fine bur. This is no longer an aggressive cutting tool, but a very fine cutting tool. Honing takes only a few seconds.

Honing will give a very fine cut. I use a diamond hone that lives on my grinder. You can make an excellent hone by gluing a sheet of 400 grit sandpaper to a piece of plywood. The diamond hone has no real advantage … except that I bought it, and by golly I am going to use it. (There have been times when I misplaced my diamond hone. No problem. I pick up a sheet of 400 grit sandpaper and lay it on a flat work place.)

Sharpening a Bowl Gouge

There are several bowl gouge sharpening jigs on the market. The only one that I really like is the David Ellsworth jig. It cost about $30 and is probably the best investment you can make in turning (next to this book of course). All jigs require some set up time to get the correct settings. This is true with the Ellsworth jig also. But once done you get the same results every time, quickly and easily.

Ellsworth Bowl Gouge Set Up

Start off by drilling a 2 inch depth hole in a block of wood next to the grinder. This is a depth gauge for the jig. You use this hole to quickly set the jig to the gouge every time you sharpen the tool. (See Figure 20.)

Figure 20. For the Ellsworth Jig start off by drilling a 1 or 2 inch depth hole in a block of wood next to the grinder. This is a depth gauge for the jig. You use this hole to quickly set the jig to the gouge every time you sharpen the tool.

Make a stop that your jig can rest in. This can be a simple "V" made from a piece of plywood. The position of the "V" is quite important. It must be 4 inches below the center of the stone and 8 inches away from the edge. Take time in getting the correct measurements. I used a pre-existing jig to get these measurements. If I was starting from scratch I would build a platform that would create the correct height of 4 inches and then I would put a plywood "V" straight out 8 inches.

Initial Sharpening of the Bowl Gouge

Put the jig on the bowl gouge and insert the gouge into the hole. Tighten the setscrew on the jig. Place the jig in the "V" and allow the tool to come into contact with the grinding stone. Slowly allow the stone to cut the tool until the sparks just barley comes over the top of the tool. Now rotate the tool to the left or the right. This creates a swept back curve that is called the "Fingernail" or "Ellsworth" grind. Do this to both sides. (See Figure 21.) Always keep the tool cool by dipping it in a bowl of water. The tip

Figure 21. Set the gouge and sharpening jig into a notch that is 4 inches below and 8 inches away from the stone.

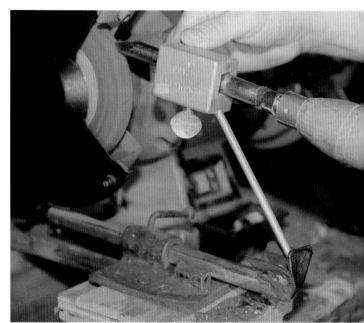

of the gouge is use to make starting cuts and roughing cuts. The side of the gouge is used to make fine shear cuts and to make big ribbons of wood come off the wood when roughing out.

Re-Sharpening Of The Bowl Gouge

Re-sharpening the bowl gouge is very quick. My Ellsworth jig lives on a stand above the grinder. When I walk up to the grinder I flip the grinder on. This allows it to come up to speed while I set the jig up. I put the jig on and insert the gouge into the hole. I tighten and set the jig into the set point. I lightly allow the tool to hit the stone. I rotate both left and right. All of this takes no more than twenty seconds in front of the grinder, but gives a beautiful edge. (See Figure 22.)

Figure 22. Once set up correctly, the Ellsworth jig will give a perfect edge every time.

Sharpening a Skew

Sharpening a skew has been considered a difficult job. You need to create a straight knife-edge on both sides of the skew. Both sides must be ground the same or it will have different cutting characteristics going from on direction to the other. In my opinion hand holding a skew to the grind stone gives a different cut on one side from the other.

The only jig that I like is the one that I make. It is called a "Flip Jig" because you sharpen one side then flip it over and grind the same edge on the opposite side. The jig works on any of the grinding platforms that are available. There does come a point though where your skew becomes too short to work with the jig

Flip Jig Set Up

The set up time for the Flip Jig is very short. Put the skew into the middle of the jig and lightly tighten the setscrews. Insert the skew into the jig and align it with the pattern that you have drawn onto your workbench. (See Figure 23.) The correct position should require you to remove a small amount of steel from the skew. Grind the edge by moving the skew back and forth across the grinding wheel. Keep the tool cool by dipping it in water. When

sparks barley come over the top along the entire edge, that side of the skew is sharp. (See Figure 24.) Flip the skew over and sharpen the other side the same way. (See Figure 25.) This edge is ready for most work. If you are going to do super fine detail work it should be buffed. The edge of the tool is buffed with a felt wheel and red rouge. Buffing is done with the felt wheel turning away from the sharp edge of the skew. Buffing requires only a few seconds. (See Figure 26.) This produces a very sharp edge. (See Figure 27.) This edge will easily shave hair off your arm.

Figure 23. To sharpen a skew, use a flip jig. The set up time for the flip jig is very short. Put the skew into the middle of the jig and lightly tighten the set screws. Insert the skew into the jig and align it with the pattern that you have drawn onto your workbench.

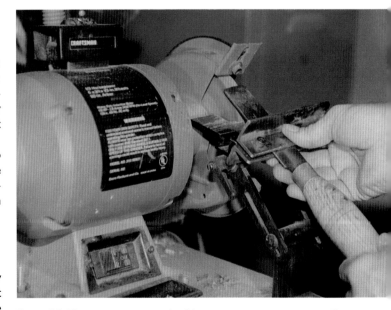

Figure 24. The correct position should require you to remove a small amount of steel from the skew. Grind the edge by moving the skew back and forth across the grinding wheel. Keep the tool cool by dipping it in water. When sparks barely come over the top along the entire edge, that side of the skew is sharp.

Figure 26. If you are going to do super fine detail work, the skew should be buffed. Buffing requires only a few seconds. The skew is being buffed against a felt wheel with red rouge. This will produce a razor sharp edge.

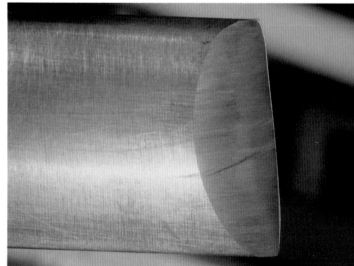

Figure 27. The flip jig, in combination with buffing, creates a razor sharp edge.

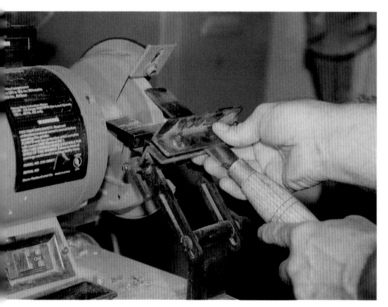

Figure 25. Flip the jig over to sharpen the other side at exactly the same angle.

Re-Sharpening The Skew

Usually I re-sharpen my skew by hand, holding it on the grinding wheel. I just barley let it touch the grinding wheel and have sparks barley come over the top edge. Then, if I want it to be razor sharp, I hone it with 400 grit sandpaper, a diamond hone, or a buffing wheel. I have a felt buffing wheel set up on one of my grinders, so that is what I usually use. Sharpening the skew and buffing it takes no more than thirty seconds.

After a while you stop testing the sharpness of your skew by shaving the hair off your arm. (Eventually there is no hair left on your arm and you give up testing it this way.) A sharp tool will drag against your fingernail, which is the way I test my tool now.

Re-Setting the Skew Edge

I can hand sharpened my skew four to six times before I find that I need to set a new edge on the skew using the Flip Jig. This takes a couple of minutes. I set the skew in the jig and line it up according to the drawing I made on my tabletop. I then tighten the two set screws. I then retouch both sides of the skew. I take the jig off and put it away. I then buff both sides of the edge for a couple of seconds.

Making a Cherry Goblet

Turned goblets can be some of the most beautiful turnings that you produce. They seem to have a universal appeal. The size and shape can vary tremendously, but should have some features in common. The cup of the goblet should be thin and delicate. The stem should be long and narrow. The base of the goblet be should about two-thirds the diameter of the widest point of the cup of the goblet. There should be transition points from the cup to the stem and from the stem to the base. The transition points are terrific opportunities for you to practice your skew work. Making this Cherry Goblet is a great learning experience and you will enjoy to fruits of your efforts for many years to come.

Choosing Wood

Find a fruitwood that is still green. Green wood cuts easily and is fun to work with. Later, in other projects, we will work with dried wood. Fruitwoods are wonderful to cut and often have beautiful color. An ice storm devastated my area in the winter of 2001. The storm was terrible. We had no electricity for a week and no water for several days. The telephones were down for two to three weeks. A lot of people stayed indoors and complained. But I immediately started collecting wood from all of the storm-damaged trees that I could. I drove all over town with my chain saw. I ended up with quite a collection of Bradford Pear and Cherry wood.

Preparing the Turning Blank

Choose a fruit limb that is about 5 inches in diameter. Cut a section 12 inches long. You can use either a chain saw or a band saw to cut the ends of the turning blank. Try to cut the ends fairly square to the long axis of the blank. This will make it a little easier for you when it is time to square up the ends of the blank. (See Figure 28.)

Figure 28. Place your turning stock between centers and lock down. Be sure to use a face shield, respirator, and apron for protection.

Mark the center of both ends. You can use a center finder, a ruler, or you can just eyeball it. Make a slight indent into both centers. I use a hammer and my live center to tap a small indent. (It would be better to use a less expensive piece of equipment to make this indent.) Place the turning blank between centers and secure in place.

Securing the Turning Blank Between Centers

The first step in this turning process is to turn the blank round and square up the ends. Turning between centers does this. The center at the headstock end is called a spur drive and it spins the turning blank. The center at the tailstock is called a live center and it allows the blank to turn without friction.

Place the turning blank between centers into the center indents at both ends. Lock the tailstock in place using the cam arm. Next use the hand wheel on the tailstock to advance the live center into the turning blank. This applies pressure to the blank and drives the blank into the spur drive. Now lock the live center into position using the lock on the side of the tailstock.

Place that tool rest in front of the turning blank at a height that makes your tool line up with the line between centers. (See Figure 28.) This height will be the starting point for all of your turning. You may decide to vary the height of the tool rest, but this is where you start.

Now hand rotate the turning blank to make sure that it does not hit the tool rest or anything else.

Setting the Speed for a Large Project

SPEED KILLS!!! The correct speed is always important in a turning project. There is always some question about what speed you should use. The faster the lathe revolves, the cleaner the cut from the tool. The slower the lathe turns, the safer the process is.

This goblet uses a very large (compared to the size of the lathe) turning blank. (See Figure 28.) The larger the turning blank the slower you need to turn. This entire goblet project will be turned at the **slowest speed** the lathe has which is **500RPM. AT NO TIME WILL A FASTER RPM BE USED!!!** Excess speed will make the turning dangerous to you and to the outcome of the project. It is also very important to always wear your face shield during turning. (See Figure 28.) **If you are too tired to wear your face shield, then you are too tired to turn. Go to the house!!**

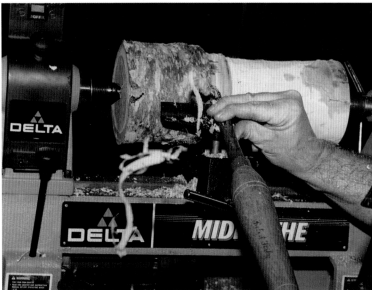

Figure 29. Use your bowl gouge to rough out the turning blank. Point the gouge straight in and take small bites.

Roughing Out the Turning Blank

A basic step in all turning is making roughing cuts to get the turning blank round. You basic bowl gouge works very well for this project. (See Figures 28-29.) Make sure that it is sharp. Put on your face shield and step away from the line of fire. Turn the lathe on to 500 RPM. There should be no vibration to the lathe. It should just run smooth. If it vibrates, it will be necessary for you to take steps to make the turning blank come into balance. This could involve: shortening the turning blank, cutting off projections, changing centers, or getting a new piece of wood.

Point your bowl gouge straight in toward the turning blank. (See Figure 29.) Advance the tip very slowly so that you are barely making contact with the wood. When the wood is not round you will be touching the wood only one time during a revolution. As the wood becomes round your tool will be making long cutting ribbons during the entire revolution. Place one hand on the tool rest to steady the tool and the other hand to the back of the handle to guide the tool. Slowly work the tool from one end of the blank to the other, making the blank into a round cylinder. (See Figure 29.) GO SLOW!! CUT GENTLE!!!

Preparing One End for a Faceplate

Turn the tailstock end of the turning blank slightly concave. (See Figure 30.) This is where you will attach your faceplate. By making it slightly concave you know that your faceplate will sit flat and not rock. You can use any straight tool of your choice for this cut: a skew, a parting tool, or a scraper.

Figure 30. Turn the tailstock end of the turning blank slightly concave. This is where you will attach your faceplate. By making it slightly concave you know that your faceplate will sit flat and not rock.

The tailstock end of the turning will be attached to a faceplate. To center the turning, it helps to leave a small nub on the tailstock end of the turning. This nub is the same size diameter as the hole in your faceplate. When you have that tailstock end of the turning on the faceplate, the nub will center the work on the faceplate. This nub will not interfere with your attaching the face-

plate, but it will help you a tremendous amount in getting the blank centered. **The more centered you are when you mount your faceplate, the less wood you will waste in getting the blank round again.**

Mounting The Faceplate

The faceplates for almost all lathes come from the factory with four holes drilled in them. **This is totally inadequate!!!** Before mounting your wood to your faceplate, it is necessary that you drill an additional four holes, evenly spaced between the existing four holes. This will give you eight screw holes, which will be adequate with the proper screw placement and cutting technique. (See Figure 31.) Use at least a 1-1/2 inch #8 metal screw to fasten the faceplate to the turning blank. I like to drive the screws in using a socket on an electric drill. Hex head screws are very nice and easy to use. They can be used over and over. (See Figure 31.) Phillips head screws strip out way too fast and should not be used.

Figure 31. Use at least a 1-1/2 inch #8 metal screw to attach the faceplate to the turning blank.

Figure 32. Mount the faceplate and turning blank onto the lathe. Then engage the live center and lock it into place. You are then ready to start shaping the goblet.

Almost all faceplates are made with four holes in them. As previously mentioned, you will need to drill four additional holes in your faceplate. The four holes may be easily drilled using a drill press or a hand held electric drill.

Screw the faceplate and turning blank onto the headstock of the lathe. Make sure that it screws all the way on. Now secure the tailstock in place and lock it in position. Hand rotate to make sure that it rotates easily. If the tailstock is not aligned straight, it will not allow the blank to rotate. If this is the case, remove the tailstock and place the tool rest in front of the tailstock dimple. With the lathe set to its lowest speed, gently re-cut the center dimples so that the live center will seat into the new center of the blank. Seat the live center into position and lock into place.

Roughing Out the Cup of the Goblet

Mark off the area for the cup of the goblet. A good measurement would be about 3 1/2 inches from the tailstock end. Use a pencil or felt tip pen to make your mark. I usually use felt tip pens because pencil lead points break too fast in my hands. Use your

Figure 35. Use calipers to make sure that the diameter of the widest part of the cup is about 3 inches.

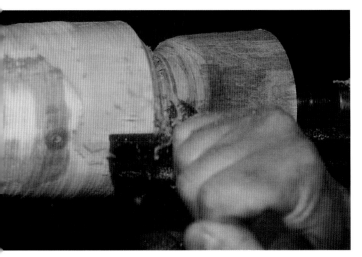

Figure 33. Use your bowl gouge to shape the cup of the goblet.

bowl gouge to rough-cut the general shape of the cup. (See Figure 32.) Use your bowl gouge to shape the cup of the goblet. (See Figure 33.) Use the side of the gouge with the top wing of the gouge almost touching the top of the bowl to make a nice finish cut. (See Figure 34.) Use calipers to make sure that the diameter of the widest part of the cup is about 3 inches. (See Figure 35.) Leave the bottom of the cup thick at this time, but go ahead and develop the general shape of the top of the cup. Leaving the base of the cup thick for now will give support to the cup while it is being hollowed out in a few minutes.

Shape the outside of the cup by using either the bowl gouge or a skew placed flat to the tool rest. At this time you are not going for an absolutely perfect finish cut on the outside of the cup. This will be done later. For now, just get a nice general shape of the cup without major cut flaws. **Remember that the base of the cup is left thick at this time to give support to the cup when the inside is hollowed out**.

Hollowing the Inside of the Cup

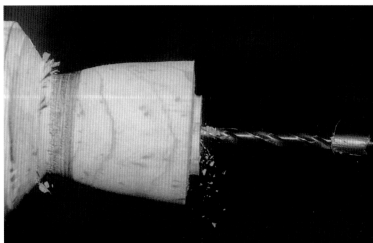

Figure 36. Drill out the center of the cup with whatever drill you have. The correct size Forstner™ bit is real nice.

Figure 34. Use the side of the gouge with the top wing of the gouge almost touching the top of the bowl to make a nice finish cut.

Hollowing out the inside of the cup must be a slow, gentle process!! Place a piece of tape onto a drill bit to mark how deep the cup will be. A good starting distance is about 3 1/4 inches depth for the cup. Drill out the center with the drill bit. (See Figure 36.) Removing the center will save you a lot of trouble when you get around to hollowing out the center of the cup. Since the speed of the center of the turning is zero, no matter how fast the rpm is — it is difficult to cut the center of the turning. When you remove the center with a drill bit, your job becomes much easier. Use the size drill bit that you have. I like a drill bit in the range of 1/4 to 1/2-inch diameter. If you are going to use

the same drill bit over and over for this job you might want to put a handle on it so that you can find it easily.

Next, rough cut the inside of the cup using a small, sharp cutting edge. (See Figures 37-38.) The cutting edge might be a: 3/8-inch bowl gouge, 3/8-inch spindle gouge, small skew, parting tool, or 3/16 cutter tip on a boring bar. **Any sharp tool will work well, if you cut slowly and gently!!**

Slowly cut from the outside of the cup toward the center. Be careful to get a good starting point on your cut so that the tool is not kicked back toward the outside edge of the cup. This will make a nasty scar in the cup, which can be difficult to correct. To get a good starting point use a sharp pointed tipped tool. Come in about 1/4-inch from the outside rim of the cup. Make a slight indentation here of about 1/8-inch. Now slowly start from this point and cut toward the center.

Cut the wall thickness a uniform 1/4-inch thick. This will be a fairly rough cut. You are not striving for perfection on this cut. **But you do want to be gentle**. The tailstock end of the turning is unsupported only during this procedure. So if you are rough, this is the point where you will tear up the project. **During all other parts of this project the goblet will be supported at both ends!!!**

Final Cut on the Inside of the Cup

The wall of the cup will be a uniform 1/4-inch thickness, except toward the bottom of the cup. Later you will reduce the outside thickness of the cup to make the cup uniform from top to bottom.

Next make finish cuts on the inside of the cup using a sharp scraper. (See Figure 39.) Get your tool rest as close as possible to the area that you are cutting. On larger projects I will put a tool rest up inside the bowl. On this project I was not able to put the tool rest that came with the Delta Midi lathe up inside the cup. Make very light cuts with the scraper and even out any irregularities that are on the inside the final inside shape and make the entire inside of the cup very smooth and even.

Figure 37. Rough out the inside of the cup with a small gouge.

Figure 38. Cut slowly from the outside toward the inside of the cup.

Figure 39. Use a sharp round nose scraper to smooth out the inside of the cup and to get the final thickness of the cup.

Figure 41. The easiest way to support the goblet is to place a soft flexible ball into the cup of the goblet. Then place the live center into the ball

Figure 40. Sand the inside of the cup. Use rough enough sandpaper to get out the cutting marks of your tool. Then sand to 400 grit sandpaper.

Now sand the inside of the cup to completion. (See Figure 40.) Use a course enough sandpaper so that you can get out all irregularities within a couple of minutes. The coarsest sandpaper you use (the first one) is the one that takes the most time. Once the first sanding is completed, the next smoother sandpaper only has to smooth down the irregularities of the sandpaper that came before it. You may start out sanding with 80 to 100 grit sandpaper. With practice you will eventually be able to start sanding in some situations at 220 sandpaper. (I did a demonstration one time where I made an outside cut and was able to start sanding at 400 grit sandpaper. Personally I can never make an inside cut that is as smooth as my outside cut. So I expect to sand a little bit more on the inside than on the outside.)

I usually sand to 800 grit. However, on this project I stopped at 320 grit because of the sandpaper that I presently have. My 400, 600, and 800 grit sandpaper is black and adds a gray color to the wood. I did not want any coloring from the sandpaper to end up on the wood on this project.

Add Finish to the Inside of the Cup

Apply finish to the inside of the cup. I use a Deft® cellulose finish that is diluted 50/50 with lacquer thinner. This is very rapid drying and gives a very good initial finish to the wood. I want some protection on the wood very quickly to keep it from drying and cracking. Apply the finish with a paper towel. Soak the wood and blot the wood with the paper towel as the wood spins. Keep the wood turning during the entire process. You do not want the finish to pool on the wood. You are not going for a final finish at this time. You just want enough finish on the wet wood to keep it from drying and cracking.

Supporting the Goblet's Free End

The inside of the cup is finished now, except for the final application of finish. It is now time to re-support the goblet from both ends and turn the remainder of the goblet. The easiest way

to support the goblet is to place a soft flexible ball into the cup of the goblet. Then place the live center into the ball. (See Figure 41.) (In this case I use my dog's glow in the dark ball. Sorry Daisy!)

Refining The Shape Of The Cup

Use your bowl gouge or skew to reduce the size of the stem of the goblet to about 1-1/2 inches. (See Figure 42.) Again it is necessary to be gentle with your cuts.

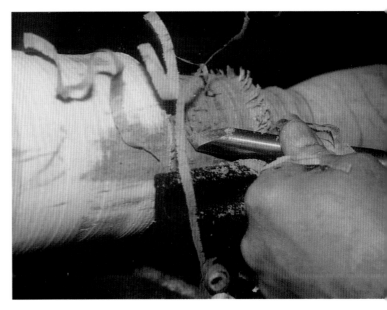

Figure 42. Use your bowl gouge or skew to reduce the size of the stem of the goblet to about 1-1/2 inches. It is necessary to be gentle with your cuts.

Mark how deep the cup goes on the outside of the goblet. (See Figure 43.) A pencil or felt marker will work well here. Use your bowl gouge to taper in the bottom of the cup so that it has a graceful curve. Stop often; remove the tailstock and the doggie ball so that you can check for thickness. Your fingers are a very accurate thickness gauge for this project.

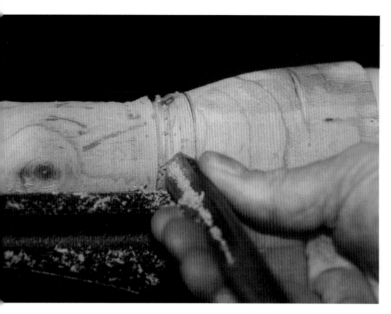

Figure 43. Use your bowl gouge to taper in the bottom of the cup so that it has a graceful curve. Stop often; remove the tailstock and the doggie ball so that you can check for thickness. Your fingers are a very accurate thickness gauge for this project.

Use your bowl gouge or skew to make a final smooth cut on the outside of the cup. (See Figure 44.) At this point the entire inside and outside shape of the cup is completed. Now sand to completion and apply finish as you did on the inside of the cup. (See Figure 45.) Remove the tailstock and the ball so that you can apply finish to both the inside and outside of the cup at the same time.

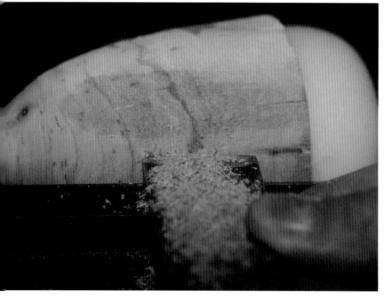

Figure 44. Use your bowl gouge or skew to make a final smooth cut on the outside of the cup. At this point the entire inside and outside shape of the cup is completed.

Cutting the Transition from the Cup to the Stem

You can make the transition of the cup to the stem as simple or as complicated as you like. For this project I choose something in the middle of the road. Not too simple and not too complicated.

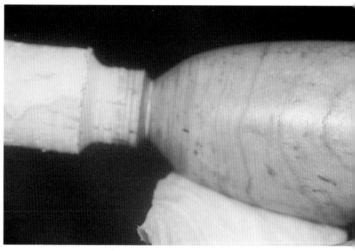

Figure 45. Sand to completion and apply finish as you did on the inside of the cup.

Make a small "V" cut at the base of the cup. (See Figure 43.) Any small pointed tool will work well. I usually use a skew. Make a small bead to set the cup apart from the stem. (See Figures 46-47.) For making small delicate cuts it is necessary that I have good lighting and good magnification. This may not be necessary for young turners.

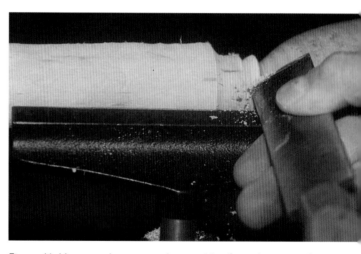

Figure 46. Use your skew to cut the transition from the cup to the stem. You can make this as simple or as complicated as you like.

Figure 47. Make a small "V" cut at the base of the cup with your skew. Make a small bead to set the cup apart from the stem. For making small delicate cuts it is necessary that I have good lighting and good magnification.

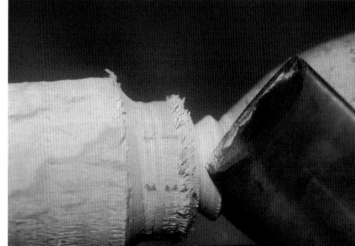

Cutting the Stem

Next cut the stem down to an approximate thickness. Decide what will be the thickest diameter of the stem. In my case, I decided that it would be 1/2-inch at the thickest point. Using your bowl gouge or skew, reduce the entire stem to the 1/2-inch thickness. (See Figure 48.) In Figure 48 I am taking a slow, gentle cut with a very sharp bowl gouge. If the stem starts to flex it will be necessary for you to support the stem with one hand while you make the cut. This is not too hard to do. Simply take two fingers that normally rest on the tool rest and put them under the tool rest and around the stem. In this way you can control the tool while supporting the stem.

Figure 48. Use your bowl gouge to reduce the thickness of the stem.

Blending the Stem to the Cup

For this stem I decided that I wanted the widest part of the stem to be in the top 1/3 of the stem. It would narrow in both directions. Moving from the widest part I used my skew to gently taper the stem toward the top and bottom of the goblet. (See Figures 49-50.)

Figure 49. Once you have the final thickness of the stem you can come back and cut the other side of your bead.

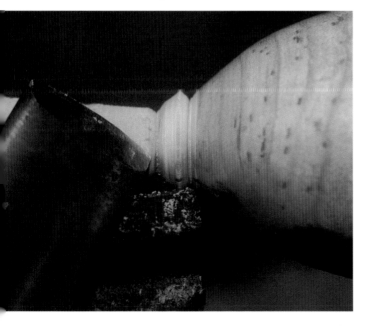

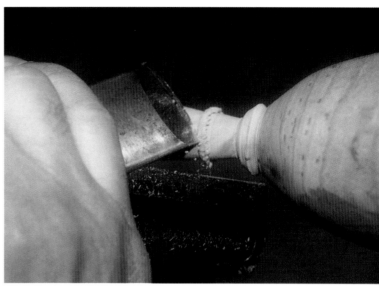

Figure 50. To make a good skew cut the blade must be up at a small angle from the wood. This takes some practice, but gives a beautiful cut.

Shaping the Base

Use a small round scraper to make the transition from the bottom of the stem to the base. (See Figure 51.) Be sure that your scraper is very sharp. Use your skew to shape the base and round over the edge of the base. (See Figure 52.) Make any small last minute refinements that are necessary at this time. The base should be about 2/3 the diameter of the widest part of the cup. The thickness of the base should be about the thickness of the widest part of the stem.

Figure 51. Blend the bottom of the stem into the base with a sharp round nose scraper. Notice that a sharp scraper can make ribbons of wood come off the turning.

Figure 52. Use your skew to shape the base of the goblet. Make small delicate cuts.

Final Sanding and Finishing

Start you parting cut at the base of the goblet. Leave about 1 inch of the support base uncut at this time. (See Figure 53.) Be sure to make the base thick enough so that the parting tool has enough room. Make the parting cut go toward the tailstock at about a 30-degree angle. This will give you a nice concave bottom that is attractive. Sand around the parting cut. Now carefully go through your final sanding process. (See Figure 54.) Take your time. This is not the time to make a mistake.

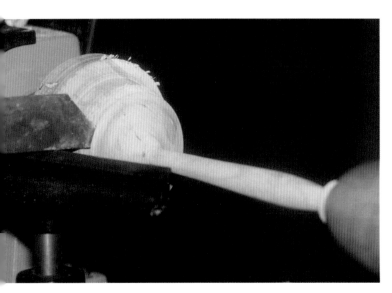

Figure 53. Shape the base of your goblet with your skew, round nose scrapper, and parting tool. Start your parting cut so that you can come back and refine around the bottom of the base.

Apply finish. Keep the lathe running as the finish dries. Make yourself comfortable and apply finish for about 30 minutes. Let the finish dry about five minutes between each application.

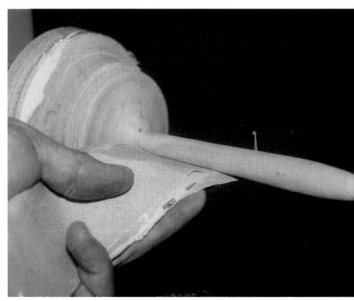

Figure 54. Sand and apply finish to the entire outside of the goblet. Sand all the way to 400 grit sandpaper. If the stem flexes while sanding, support the back of the stem with a couple of your fingers.

Parting Off

Part the goblet off using a thin parting tool, like the Chris Scott parting tool. Remove the tailstock and hold the goblet with the right hand. Use your left hand to make the parting cut.

Carefully trim the nub from the bottom of the goblet with a sharp knife or carving tool. Sand the bottom and apply finish.

Congratulations!! You have just created a beautiful turning that you and your family will enjoy for years.

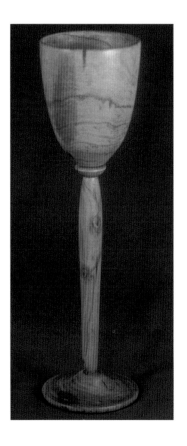

Mushroom Magic

Part 1—Turning with a 4-Jaw Chuck

Turned wooden mushrooms are fun, beautiful, and popular!! They can also be a good source of income. Women and children seem to be especially attracted to them. Turning mushrooms develops a lot of turning skill that will come in handy in all of your other turning projects.

Choice of Wood

Use small limbs 5 inches in diameter or smaller. This is a great way to get rid of limbs in your woodpile that are too small to make into a bowl. Use whatever wood you have. Fruitwood is nice. Try to stay way from very soft wood like pine. Cut the limbs into sections 10 inches long. This is a good exercise to use wet wood. It will crack later when it dries, but the cracks look just like the cracks that appear in real mushrooms.

Lathe Speed And Safety

The lathe speed for this entire project will be the minimum speed of the lathe, which is 500 RPM. Do not go above this speed. You are turning a long project that could get out of balance and go flying. Remember!!! Always wear a face shield!!

Getting Started

Cut a piece of wet fruitwood about 5 inches in diameter and about 10 inches long. Put it between the centers. (See Figure 55.) Advance that live center into the turning blank and lock the live center in place. Adjust your tool rest so that the turning blank will not hit the wood when it revolves. Set the lathe to its lowest speed, 500 RPM. Put your face shield on and step out of the line of fire when your turn the lathe on.

Figure 55. Mount a piece of wet wood between centers. Be sure to lock the tailstock in place.

Sharpen your bowl gouge before starting this project. Use your sharp bowl gouge to rough turn the turning blank. (See Figure 56.) To get rid of the bark, slowly push the tip straight into the wood. After you get rid of the unevenness, you can do a shear cut by rubbing the side bevel of the tool against the turning blank. This makes very nice ribbons of wet wood fly off. To do this, the tool rest must be very close to the turning blank and you must be rubbing both the front and back edge (this is called rubbing the bevel) of the tool on the wood.

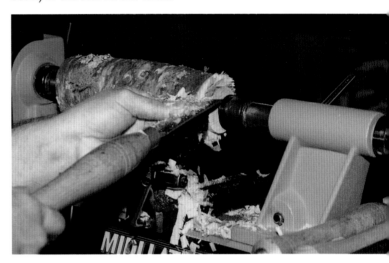

Figure 56. Cut a spigot that will fit into your 4-jaw chuck. The shoulders of the spigot must rest on the top of the jaws. This means that the spigot must be shorter than the jaws are deep.

Cutting a Spigot

For a 4-jaw chuck to work, it must have a good shoulder and tenon to hold to. The tenon must be just slightly shorter then the depth of the jaws of the chuck. (See arrow in Figure 57.) The caliper is set to the depth of the jaws in the 4-jaw chuck. Then the tenon is cut to be just a little bit shorter. This means that the turning blank shoulder rests on the lip of the 4-jaw chuck. This shoulder on the lip gives much more stability then you get if you only use a tenon without a shoulder.

Figure 57. Use a set of calipers to measure the diameter of the 4-jaw chuck when it is almost closed. This will be the diameter of the spigot. Also measure the depth of the jaws. The tenon must be a little shorter than this measurement.

Mounting/Using a 4-Jaw Chuck

Place the turning blank in the jaws and in the live center of the tailstock. (See Figure 58.) Tighten the 4-jaw chuck. Be sure to remove the key from the 4-jaw chuck before you turn the lathe on.

Figure 58. Mount your 4-jaw chuck and your turning blank on the lathe. Tighten the jaws down onto the spigot. Make sure that the spigot is firmly seated.

Roughing Out

Use your bowl gouge to rough out the turning blank. (See Figure 59.) Use the lowest RPM that you can, which is 500 RPM. Be sure to have your face shield on.

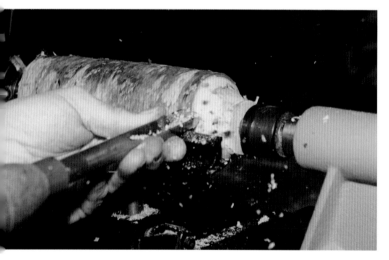

Figure 59. Use your bowl gouge to rough out the turning blank. Use the lowest RPM that you can, which is 500 RPM. Be sure to have your face shield on.

Cutting the Cap of the Mushroom

Cut the cap of the mushroom using a bowl gouge. Mushrooms come in all shapes, so have fun making different shape mushroom caps. Start using your bowl gouge. If you have a small bowl gouge, you might want to use it to make a little "V" to separate the top of the mushroom from the tip of the live center. (See Figure 60.) Continue to shape the cap of the mushroom with your regular size gouge. (See Figure 61.)

Figure 60. Use a small tool like a small bowl gouge to make a little "V" to separate the top of the mushroom from the tip of the live center

Figure 61. Use your regular size bowl gouge or skew to shape the top of the mushroom cap.

Roughing Out the Stem and Base

Use your bowl gouge to rough out the shape of the entire mushroom. (See Figures 62-64.) Use your skew to flatten out the stem and to make it even. (See Figure 63.) For this cut the skew is rested flat on the tool rest. This is a safe scraping cut made with the skew flat on the tool rest. Shape the foot of the mushroom with your bowl gouge. (See Figure 64.) Make small, slow, and gentle cuts.

Figure 62. Use your bowl gouge to "rough out" the stem of the mushroom. This is fun because you can let the chips fly!

Figure 63. Use your skew held flat to shape the stem and to bring it to final thickness.

Figure 64. Use your bowl gouge to rough shape the base of the mushroom.

Transition from Stem to Base

Making a smooth transition from the stem to the cap or to the base can be difficult. A small round nose scraper makes this much easier. A very sharp scraper can cut a fine ribbon shaving. (See Figure 65.)

Figure 65. Use your scraper to blend the stem into the base. Notice that the scraper makes nice shavings.

Shaping the Base

Use your bowl gouge to rough shape the base. (See Figure 66.) Use your skew and round nose scraper to finish shaping the base.

Figure 66. Use your bowl gouge to remove waste wood at the base of the turning.

Parting Off the Tailstock Nub

Part off the tailstock nub. You can do this in several ways. The simplest way is to use a thin parting tool. I usually like to use a small bowl gouge to remove most of the waste wood. (See Figure 67.) I then start using a small round skew to deepen the "V". (See Figure 68.) I make the final parting cut with the small round skew. This makes a nice smooth surface. (See Figure 69.) You can just as easily use your regular skew for this step.

Figure 67. Use your parting tool to cut in where the bottom of the base will be. Round this area over with a skew or bowl gouge.

Sanding

Sand to 400 grit at this stage. Get rid of all imperfections in cutting. (See Figure 70.) If you have any ripples in the wood, get rid of them now. Start with a grit sandpaper that is rough enough to sand out the imperfections within a minute or two. If it takes any longer than this, you should use rougher sandpaper. Getting out the ripples with the first sandpaper is the slowest part of sanding. All subsequent sandpapers go very fast because they only have to take out the ripples of the previous sandpaper.

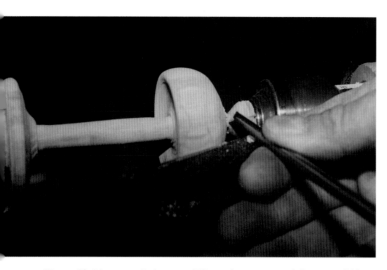

Figure 68. Use a small sharp tool like a skew or round skew to nibble away at the nub at the top of the mushroom cap. Here I am using a 1/4-inch round skew, but I could have used a small skew just as well.

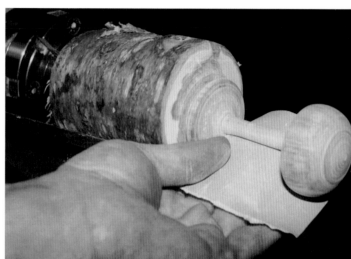

Figure 70. Sand the entire mushroom. Use a course enough grit sandpaper to get out all of the tool marks within two to four minutes. Sand all the way to 400 grit sandpaper.

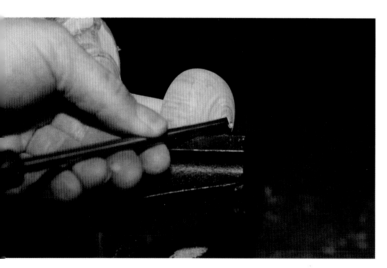

Figure 69. Use a sharp edge to make the final cut on the top of the mushroom. You can use a gouge, or skew, or scraper. Here I used a 1/4-inch round skew that I make.

Applying Finish

Rub on your finish at this stage. I like to use Deft cellulose finish diluted 50/50 with lacquer thinner. Apply with paper towels. This is a very nice finish that dries very quickly. (See Figure 71.) **Never, Never, Never use cloth around a lathe!!!!!** If the cloth grabs, it can pull you into the lathe or pull a finger or arm off.

Figure 71. Apply finish while the mushroom is still on the lathe. A mixture of cellulose finish diluted 50/50 with lacquer thinner makes a nice finish.

Parting Off

Use your thin parting tool to cut the mushroom off. (See Figure 72.) Be careful! You might want to use a thin saw blade to make the final part of the cut. Sand off the bottom by hand sanding. Then apply finish and hand rub in.

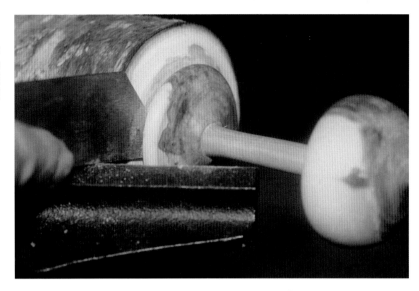

Figure 72. Part off the mushroom with a thin parting tool. Sand the bottom and apply finish.

Conclusion

Congratulations! You have just turned a mushroom. Your friends and family will enjoy the mushroom and you have gained a lot of turning experience.

Figure 73. Mushrooms are fun projects and make great gifts.

Mushroom Magic

Part 2 — Eccentric Turning with a Face Plate

You can use your newly acquired mushroom turning skills to do a more advanced eccentric turning. In this exercise we will do an eccentric turned mushroom. The turned mushroom after a bit of sanding becomes a beautiful turned and carved (turned/carved) work of art. In the past, most eccentric turning was done with a $300 eccentric chuck. I figured out a safe and free way for you to use your faceplate to get the same results. So let's have some fun developing some new turning skills while making a sculptured turning.

Getting Started

Cut a piece of wet fruitwood about 5 inches in diameter and about 8 inches long and put it between centers. (See Figure 74.) Advance that live center into the turning blank and lock the live center in place. Adjust your tool rest so that the turning blank will not hit the wood when it revolves. Set the lathe to its lowest speed, 500 RPM. Put your face shield on and step out of the line of fire when your turn the lathe on.

Figure 74. Cut a piece of wet fruitwood about 5 inches in diameter and about 10 inches long. Put it between centers. Advance that live center into the turning blank and lock the live center in place. Adjust your tool rest so that the turning blank will not hit the wood when it revolves.

Sharpen your bowl gouge before starting this project. Use your sharp bowl gouge to rough turn the turning blank. (See Figure 75.) To get rid of the bark, slowly push the tip straight into the wood. After you get rid of the unevenness, you can do a shear cut by rubbing the side bevel of the tool against the turning blank. This makes very nice ribbons of wet wood fly off. (See Figure 75.) To do this, the tool rest must be very close to the turning blank and you must be rubbing both the front and back edge of the gouge (this is called rubbing the bevel) on the wood.

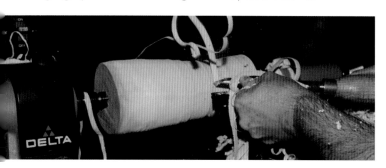

Faceplate Basics

Cut the tailstock end of the turning blank slightly concave. This ensures that the faceplate will sit flat. (See Figure 76.) You can use any tool of choice. Here I am using a 1/2-inch skew. Use your calipers to leave a very short nub in the center of the blank that is the same diameter as the inside of your faceplate. This short nub will ensure that your faceplate is centered when you mount it. (See Figure 77.) You can later remove the nub with a hammer and chisel if it is in the way.

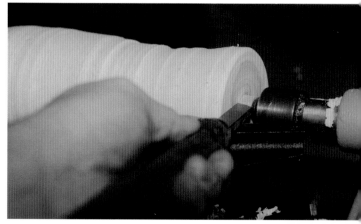

Figure 76. Make a short nub the same diameter as the hole in your faceplate. This will help you center your faceplate.

Figure 77. Attach the faceplate to the turning blank with eight 1-1/2 inch hex drive metal screws.

Attach the faceplate to the turning blank with eight 1-1/2 inch hex drive metal screws. (See Figures 77-78.) I like to use an electric drill with a socket attachment for this job because it saves time and wear and tear on my hands. Mount the faceplate on the lathe and bring the tailstock into position and lock it. Advance the live center into the wood and lock the live center. **This is your basic faceplate mounting technique**. You will use this basic technique for all of your faceplate work!!!

Figure 75. After you get rid of the unevenness, you can do a shear cut by rubbing the side bevel of the tool against the turning blank. This makes very nice ribbons of wet wood fly off.

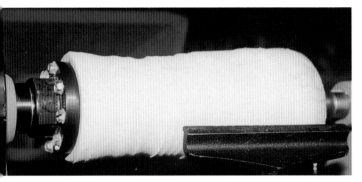

Figure 78. Mount the faceplate and turning blank on your lathe. Set the tailstock and lock it in place. Advance the live center and secure it.

Cutting the Cap of the Mushroom

Cut the cap of the mushroom the way you did in Part 1. Start using your bowl gouge and then finish using your skew. (See Figure 79.) Sand the cap of the mushroom to completion. (See Figure 80.) You will not be able to return to this stage on the lathe later. It is now or never. Apply any stain to the cap now if you want to use stain. (See Figure 81.) Here I used Rit™ cloth dye. Be sure to put some type of protection on the lathe to protect it from stain splatter. In this case I used an old towel because it was handy.

Figure 79. Cut the cap of your mushroom with a bowl gouge and then complete the finish cut with a skew.

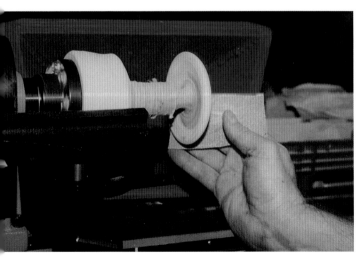

Figure 80. Sand the top and bottom of the cap at this time.

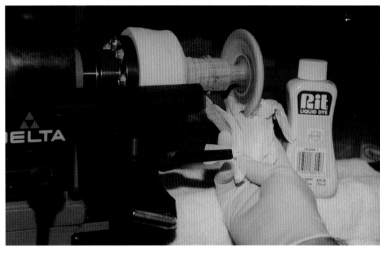

Figure 81. Apply dyes if you want to. Be sure to put down a drop cloth when you use dyes.

Preparing for Eccentric Faceplate Turning

Number each hole on the faceplate 1 to 8. I used a piece of red electrical tape and a permanent marker. Next number the hole locations on the turning blank 1 to 8. **Throughout this entire project, the hole location on the faceplate will always align with the original hole in the turning blank.** Number 1 faceplate hole will always go into #1 hole of the wood.

Now take the faceplate off the lathe and remove the 8 screws. This is where you will see the value of the electric drill and the socket drive. Insert a 3/8-inch-thick spacer between the faceplate and the turning blank at the #1 screw position. The spacer can be a nut or several washers put together. (See Figure 82.) Re-tighten the 8 screws.

Figure 82. The first offset is created by placing a 3/8-inch spacer between the face plate and the turning at the No.1 hole position.

There are 8 screws and you will repeat this procedure 8 times. When you count the original mounting of the faceplate, your will be driving in 72 screws and removing 72 screws. This is why the electric drill becomes so nice.

Eccentric Turning

This is where the excitement begins!! You are about to turn something that is out of round. There are several safety precautions that are very important. Position the tool rest and make sure that the wood can revolve. **You must hand rotate!!** You cannot do this by the "eye ball" technique. While the backside might clear the tool rest, the front side might rotate over and bang into the tool rest.

Make sure your speed is still set to its lowest speed of 500 RPM. Put on your face shield. Stand clear and turn on the lathe. The mushroom will be "wobbling" as it turns. (See Figure 83.) Make an initial cut at the stem close to the cap of the mushroom. Ease your cut forward toward the cap of the mushroom. Stop often to make sure that you are not cutting the stem too thin. (See Figure 84.) In this photograph the spacer is in the #2 position and I am making my second eccentric cut.

Figure 83. Make sure your tool rest clears the offset turning. Do not let your finger get caught. Cut slowly and check often.

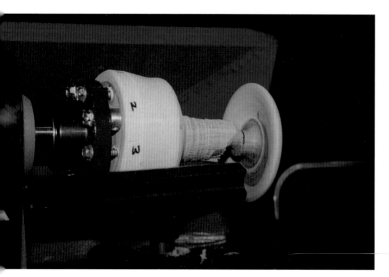

Figure 84. Check to see how much you have cut off. It is easy to cut too much.

If you are satisfied that you have cut enough at the #1 position, move your spacer to the #2 screw hole. (See Figure 84.) Make your second eccentric cut a little closer to the base than the first one. (See Figure 85.) Again check often to make sure that you do not remove too much from the stem. Progress in this way all the way through to the number 8 screw. (See Figure 86; in this photograph the spacer is now in the #7 position.) With each eccentric cut we will move our gouge closer to the headstock, or base of the mushroom.

Figure 85. Move the spacer to the No.2 hole position and make your second cut a little closer toward the headstock. With each change in the spacer you will cut a new section which is closer to the headstock than the one before.

Figure 86. The spacer has been in positions 1 to 6. It is now in the No. 7 position, ready to go.

Finishing The Base

Leave the spacer in the #8 position. (See Figure 87.) This will make the cap of the mushroom tilt at an angle. If you do not want the cap of the mushroom to be tilted then remove the spacer to finish the base. Start shaping the base. I used a small bowl gouge for this job, but you can use whatever feels good to you. (See Figure 87.) A scraper or a skew would work equally well.

Open up a large working area below the base. This is to allow you to get your parting tool into this area safely. (See Figure 88.) Also, it allows you to do some sanding of the base.

Notice that the transition from one cut to the next is rough. (An arrow marks this area.) This will have to be sanded after the mushroom is parted off. (See Figure 88.)

Figure 87. The space has been in all 8 positions and now the base is being cut. By leaving the spacer in when the base is cut the cup will be tilted when it is finished.

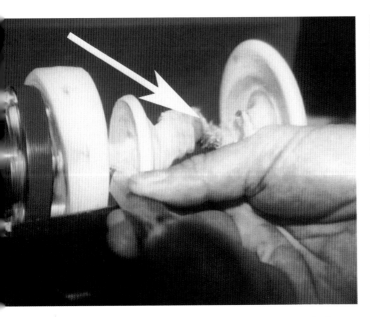

Figure 88. Use a wide parting tool to open up a space under the base of the mushroom. Notice at the arrow that the eccentric cuts are rough.

Parting Off

Use your thin parting tool to cut the mushroom off. (See Figure 89.) Be careful! You might want to use a thin saw blade to make the final part of the cut.

Figure 89. Part off using a thin parting tool. You may want to saw through the last little bit of the tenon.

Shaping with a Small Drum Sander

Use a small drum sander to shape the eccentric stem. I used a 3/4-inch rough grit (80 grit) drum sander to do my shaping. (See Figure 90.) When sanding it is very important to control the dust. When I sand I have a fan behind me blowing the dust away and a 4-inch vacuum picking up dust from the sander. In addition, I used a respirator any time I make any fine dust. Get comfortable and take your time shaping the stem. This is a form of carving; and carving takes time. However, the results will be worth the effort.

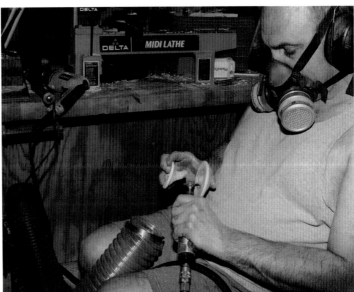

Figure 90. Use a drum sander to blend all of the cuts together. I used an air powered die grinder, but you could use a Dremel™ or Foredom™ handpiece. Be sure to use good dust control.

Sanding and Finishing the Bottom

Use a round padded sanding disc to sand the bottom of the mushroom. Start with a course grit to remove the parting tool marks. Then progress all the way to fine grit sandpaper. (See Figure 91.)

Hand apply the finish of your choice.

Figure 91. I like to sand the bottom of my bowls with hook and loop sandpaper. It is a very quick and efficient way to take care of a bottom. Notice that my dust is going straight into the 4-inch vacuum tube.

Conclusion

Eccentric turning has a lot of applications that you will slowly discover. Using your faceplate for eccentric turning is a nice inexpensive way to create some beautiful and unusual turnings. It can give your work a very distinctive hand carved appearance. Eccentric turned mushroom are fun and attractive. You will have a lot of fun making them and your loved ones will enjoy your efforts for years to come.

Figures 92a-g. You can get a very nice sculptured look for eccentric turning. You might even grow a "garden" of turned mushrooms!

Figure 92c

Figure 92a

Figure 92b

Figure 92d

Figure 92e

Figure 92f

Figure 92g

Eight-Inch-Diameter Walnut Bowl
with Turquoise Inlay
Introduction

Bowls were one of the first inventions of ancient man. Bowls were originally made of bone, or clay, or wood. Later bowls were made from metal or porcelain. The bowl's first use was utilitarian but esthetics very quickly became important. Eventually beautiful bowls were made solely for the purpose of art. Beautiful bowls are still popular. They are one of the most popular items that a turner produces. In the following exercise, we will learn how to make a basic bowl and then embellish it with a commercially available turquoise inlay material called Inlace™.

Wood Preparation

For this project we will be working with dried wood. I want you to learn how to work not only with wet wood but also with dry wood. Both wet and dry woods have advantages and disadvantages. Wet wood is easy and fun to cut. Very often wet wood is free and you can get wet wood in any size that you want.

Dry wood is usually expensive because you have to buy it. There is a limit to how thick wood can be dried. The thickest dry wood that I have ever found measures 4 inches, which is what I am using for this project. You will probably use 3-inch thick stock, which is available from turning supply stores.

I used 40-year-old air-dried walnut. It was 12 inches wide and 4 inches thick when I bought it from an old woodturner friend. He had it stored in his shop for 40 years and finally decided that he was not going to make a gunstock out of it.

I first used a thickness planer to get one side smooth. I then cut the wood into 12-inch by 12-inch sections. This was heartwood and had a lot of cracks that went almost all the way through the wood. In the drying process the wood had cracked a lot. It was necessary for me to cut away part of the cracks from my blank to eliminate the biggest of the cracks. But I paid a lot of money for this wood and I wanted to use it.

Start off by gluing a 3/4-inch thick piece of plywood to the smooth side of the turning blank. I like to use yellow glue. (See Figure 93.) Yellow glue is inexpensive and works well if you give it 24 hours to set. Do not use less time than the manufacturer recommends. They have a vested interest in recommending the correct set up time. They want their product to work for you.

Use a straight edge and a pencil to draw diagonal lines from corner to corner on the plywood. This will quickly give you the center of the block. Now use your compass to draw a circle. Cut the turning block round on a band saw. (See Figure 94.) This allows you to get the largest piece possible on your lathe. I had to cut away some weak cracked wood. Therefore my diameter was reduced to 8 1/8 inches instead of a 10-inch maximum diameter.

Figure 94. Mark the center of the bowl by drawing cross lines from corner to corner. Then use your band saw to cut the blank round. (If you do not have a band saw that is okay. Just slowly knock off the corners on the lathe.) Attach the faceplate with 8 7/8-inch long screws.

Attach your faceplate with eight 5/8-inch long screws. On my faceplate this meant that the screws just barely stayed in the plywood. To make mounting the faceplate easier, draw a circle on the plywood to show you the correct placement of the faceplate. This will allow very accurate placement of the faceplate.

Place the turning blank on the headstock and tighten down. Put the tailstock into place and lock down. Advance the live cen-

Figure 93. Glue a piece of 3/4-inch plywood to the back of your dried turning blank. Allow the yellow glue to dry overnight. Place a drop cloth of some type underneath to decrease the mess on your table.

ter into top of bowl and lock it down for safety. Hand-rotate the turning blank to make sure it clears the tool rest. (See Figure 95.) The arrow points to the turning blank clearing the tool rest.

Now sharpen your bowl gouge. (See Figure 95.) You will be cutting very dry and therefore very hard wood. You will need to re-sharpen your tool numerous times during the turning process.

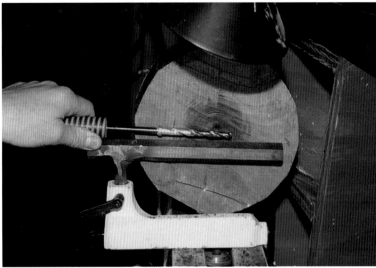

Figure 96. Make a slight dimple in the center of the bowl so that your drill bit has a starting point. Make a mark on your drill bit that indicates how deep you want to cut. Make sure your bowl gouge is sharp. Drill to your initial depth using your drill bit.

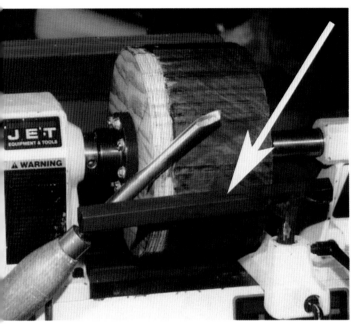

Figure 95. Hand rotate the turning blank to make sure it clears the tool rest. The arrow points to the turning blank clearing the tool rest.

Tool Rest

My tool rest broke shortly after I got my mini lathe. I do not like cast iron tool rests because they break easily and the broken edge can be dangerous. Therefore, I make all of my tool rests from steel, which can be bent but not broken. If you would like to order a tool rest from me, see the section on tool rests on page 8.

For this project it was necessary to make an additional tool rest that would reach across the entire length of the bowl. (See arrow in Figure 95.) I made a 10-inch asymmetrical 1-inch thick hex steel tool rest. It is 9 inches long on one side of the tool rest and 1 inch long on the other. This allowed me to get to all of the positions that the regular tool rest would not allow me to get to.

Initial Cuts

If you did not have a band saw to cut the piece round, then you will need to spend a few minutes turning the outside diameter round. Use a bowl gouge to turn the blank round.

Usually we cut the outside shape of a bowl first. However in this case we will be cutting the inside of the bowl first. In this way we will have the full support of the plywood glue block and we should have no problem with the glue joint letting go. (See Figure 95.)

You will hear other teachers talk about using paper joints between the plywood and the turning blank. And others will say that you need to let the glue dry for only one hour. This may work for you later, when your skill level is higher, but please do not try it now. I have had these joints let go on me and destroy the project. (And scare the stuffing out of me!!!)

Cutting the Inside

Make a slight dimple in the center of the bowl so that your drill bit has a starting point. Make a mark on your drill bit to indicate how deep you want to cut. (See Figure 96.) I wanted an initial depth of 3 inches on a 4-inch bowl. This gives me plenty of room to sand the inside of the bowl and make a nice reverse turned bottom on the base of the bowl. I will probably end up with a bottom that is 3/8 to 1/2-inch thick. But I want some flexibility at the beginning.

Drill to your initial depth using your drill bit. (See Figure 96.) Then use a parting tool to make your initial cut at what will be the outside of the bowl area. (See Figure 97.) This will help prevent your bowl gouge from kicking back as you start your cut. With a little practice, this step will not be necessary. Now use your bowl gouge to cut the inside of the bowl.

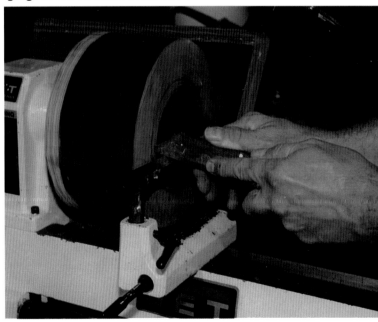

Figure 97. Use a parting tool to make your initial cut at what will be the outside of the bowl area. This will help prevent your bowl gouge from kicking back as you start your cut. With a little practice this step will not be necessary.

Start from the outside of the bowl area and work your way toward the center. (See Figure 98.) You will notice a red circle on the walnut. I very often use a red or black marker, or a piece of chalk, to mark the area that needs to be worked on. This saves me a lot of time by making me take off enough wood in the area that needs cutting. Position your tool rest close to where you are working. Make shallow cuts. This dry wood is very hard. It is slow to cut and is hot when it hits your finger. (You will notice in Figures 104-105 that I got tired of having my fingers burned and put on some gloves.) Continue shaping the round inside bowl area.

Figure 98. Use your bowl gouge to cut the inside of the bowl. Start from the outside of the bowl area and work your way toward the center.

Treating Weak Wood

Sometimes you can save cracked wood by reinforcing it with cyano-acrylic glue. My wood had large cracks that were likely to cause the bowl to come apart during the turning process. I took the wood off the lathe and poured cyano-acrylic glue into the cracks. The glue was leaking out the sides, so I sprayed accelerator onto the sides. This created a dam to help hold the glue in the area where I needed it. This technique requires a lot of cyano-

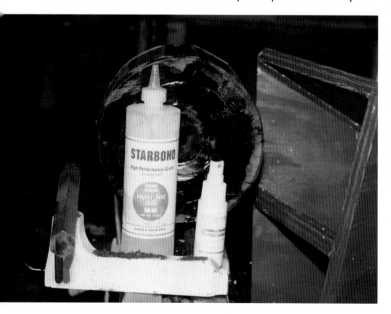

acrylic glue. I buy my glue in pint bottles. (See Figure 99.) This works well for me. The bottle last a long time and I do not have trouble with it going bad too fast. This bottle has presently been in use for nine months, which is a long time for cyano-acrylic glue.

Refining the Inside Shape

Once you have most of the wood cut out you can start refining the inside shape. To do this I use my bowl gouge on its edge. (See Figure 100.) I start at the center of the bowl and scrape backwards toward the outside edge. This gives a nice finish cut. Also a scraper works very well for making a final shaping and final finish cut. (See Figure 101.)

Figure 100. You can use your bowl gouge with a powerful back scraping motion to remove a large amount of wood in a hurry. Here I am cutting from the center back to the outside of the bowl.

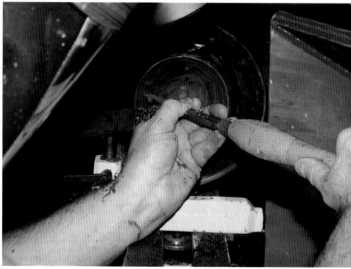

Figure 101. A scraper works very well for making a final shaping and final finish cut. The tool is easy to control and does a great job.

Figure 99. Sometimes you can save cracked wood by reinforcing it with cyano-acrylic glue.

Flatten the Rim

Use your bowl gouge to flatten the top of the rim. (See Figure 102.) It took me several steps to get cyano-acrylic glue into all of the cracks. I would allow this to harden or use an accelerator if necessary and then re-cut the rim to get it flat.

Figure 102. Flatten the rim with your bowl gouge. Be sure to have the tool rest very close to the work area.

Set the Initial Rim Thickness

Mark off the initial rim thickness with your parting tool. Make it thick at this time. A thickness of 1/2-inch would be a good starting thickness. Use a parting tool to mark the initial thickness of the rim. (See Figure 103.)

Figure 103. Mark off the initial rim thickness with your parting tool. Make it thick at this time. A thickness of 1/2-inch would be for a start. Use a parting tool to mark the initial thickness of the rim

Notice that I have a firm grip on my parting tool. On a couple of occasions when I had a light grip, the wood grabbed the tool and caused a catch. When the tool slapped down onto the tool rest, my finger was underneath it. I received a real good pinched finger.

You will thin the rim down later. But you need the initial thickness for several reasons. First, all of the cutting that you are doing on the bowl will release stresses that were built up in the wood while the tree was growing. The rim will warp some during the turning process and you need room to be able to make it flat again. Second, you need some thickness for artistic control. You need to be able to make some initial cut to try different designs. And you need to be able to go back and remove mistakes.

Cutting the Rim

Use your bowl gouge to remove a large amount of wood below the rim. (See Figures 104-105.) After you get used to handling your bowl gouge it may not be necessary for you to make the initial cut with the parting tool. After all the years that I have been turning, I sometimes still like to make the starter cut with the parting tool. This technique is especially important if I am in a delicate situation where I cannot afford a spiral kick back with the bowl gouge. (Most turners fear the spiral kick back of the skew, but the spiral kick back of the bowl gouge can be a nuisance also. This gouge kickback will not be a problem for you because you now know how to make the parting cut first. As far as I know I am the inventor of this technique. However, my friend Gorst Duplessis is quick to point out, "There is nothing new under the sun."

Figure 104. Use your bowl gouge to remove a large amount of wood below the rim.

Figure 105. Use your bowl gouge to start cutting the general shape of the bowl. Be sure to leave the base very wide at this time so that the glue joint will remain strong.

Shaping the Bottom of the Bowl

Use your bowl gouge to remove a large amount of wood toward the bottom of the bowl. Since I made the inside of the bowl round, I decided to make the outside of the bowl round. (See Figures 105-106.) Usually I like to make the outside shape of the bowl like the Roman Ogee curve. (This is a popular shape for router bits to cut molding.) Leave the bottom of the bowl a little thick at this time so that there will be enough glue support so that the face plate glue joint will not break. Refine the bottom's shape with a skew or gouge. (See Figure 106.)

Figure 106. Use your skew to refine the shape of the bowl. The skew lying flat on its side produces a scraping cut. It is not the best cut in the world but it is an easy to control cut.

Shape the Bottom Side of the Rim

Use your bowl gouge to shape the bottom side of the rim. (See Figure 107.) The bowl gouge is turned up on its side for this cut. Be careful not to get the rim too thin at this time. You need thickness so that you will be able to work on the top side of the rim.

Figure 107. Use your bowl gouge to shape the bottom side of the rim. The bowl gouge is turned up on its side for this cut.

Shape the Top of the Rim

Set your tool rest in front of the rim. The rim should have warped a little bit while you were working on the bottom of the bowl. This warping has nothing to do with moisture content. My wood had been air-drying for 40 years. The warping is a result of internal stresses being released during the cutting process. Flatten the rim again using your bowl gouge. (See Figure 102.)

Blend the top edge to the bottom edge with either your bowl gouge or your skew. Use whatever sharp pointed tool you have to make some coves on the top of the rim. I used a sharp pointed spindle gouge and a skew to form little round beds on the inside and outside of the rim. (See Figures 108-109.)

Figure 108. Use whatever sharp pointed tool you have to make some coves on the top of the rim. I used a sharp pointed spindle gouge and a skew to form little round beds on the inside and outside of the rim

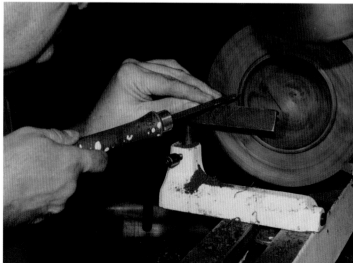

Figure 109. Make 2 small coves on the inside and outside of the rim. Next cut a 1/2-inch trough in the middle of the rim for your turquoise inlay. Use a sharp skew for this.

Next cut a 1/2-inch trough in the middle of the rim for your turquoise inlay. Use a sharp skew for this. Be sure to get it deep enough so that there is adequate inlay material. A depth of 1/8 inch should be enough. (See Figure 110.)

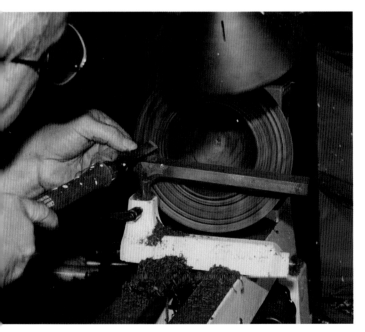

Figure 110. Use very precise hand control to make good beads.

Figure 112. Mix the material and hardener well in the paper cup with the wooden stick that is provided. Add turquoise to the material now if you like. Use the stirring stick to place the inlay material into the channel that you cut

At this point I used a very sharp round nose scraper to make the bowl area very round and very smooth. (See Figure 111.)

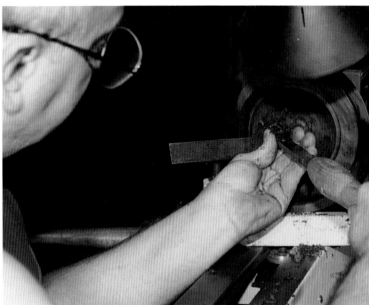

Figure 111. Use a very sharp round nose scraper to make the bowl area very round and very smooth

Placing the Inlay Material

Take your bowl off the lathe and set it upright. This is a good working position and you should not have a problem with your inlay material running. You can use crushed turquoise and cyano-acrylic glue to make a nice inlay. In this project I use "Inlace" Inlay Material. It is a very nice plastic material that comes in very many different colors and textures.

I chose the material "Lacey"™ because it was close in appearance to the "turquoise" that was provided in my kit.

Follow the instructions that come with the kit. For this procedure you will need about 2 ounces of inlay material and about 1-1/2 capfuls of hardener. Mix the material and hardener well in the paper cup with the wooden stick that is provided. (See Figure 112.) Add turquoise to the material now if you like.

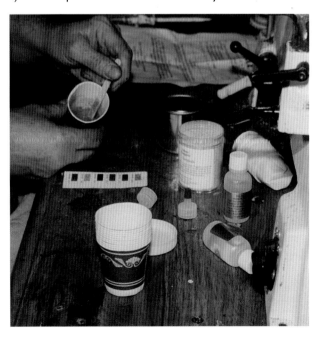

37

Use the stirring stick to place the inlay material into the channel that you cut. If you did not add enough turquoise to the mix, you can do so now. (See Figure 113.) Allow the plastic inlay to harden for 24 hours.

Figure 113. Add additional turquoise to the resin if you did not add enough.

Finishing the Inlace Inlay

Use your sharp bowl gouge on its side to cut the inlay material flat after it has hardened. (See Figure 114.) Use a sharp pointed skew or gouge to re-cut your beads. (See Figure 115.) I used a sharp pointed shallow gouge for this procedure. This is the tool that I go to when I am nervous and need to make a "sure fire" delicate cut. I may *only* start the cut with this tool, but I get the cut started with it. It is my "security blanket" tool for delicate situations. Your special "Go To" tool may be anything that you trust to carry you through an important or delicate situation.

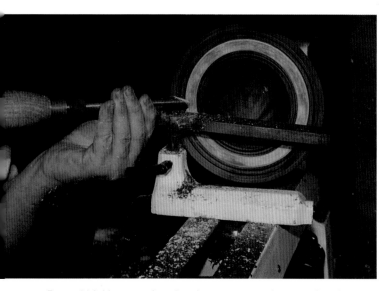

Figure 114. Use your sharp bowl gouge on its side to cut the inlay material flat after it has hardened.

Figure 115. Use a sharp pointed skew or gouge to re-cut your beads.

I only sharpen my blue handle 3/8-inch shallow gouge about every two weeks. This shows that I do not cut much with it. But 4 seconds of cutting with it often makes it safe for me to start cutting with another tool. For comparison I sharpen my bowl gouge about every 7 minutes of cutting. And I will always re-sharpen to make a finish cut.

Sanding

Sand the bowl while it is on the lathe. I like to go to 800 grit. But at this time my 600 and 800 grit sandpaper is black and marks the wood. So I only sanded to 400 grit. (See Figure 116.) Be sure to sand all areas, including the small troughs in between the coves.

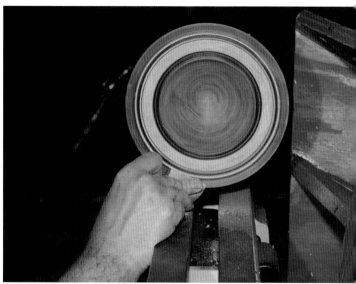

Figure 116. Sand the bowl while it is on the lathe. Be sure to sand all areas, including the small troughs in between the coves.

Applying Finish

Use a paper towel to apply a very quick drying finish to the bowl. (See Figure 117.) For this project I used a 50/50 mixture of Deft cellulose finish diluted with lacquer thinner. It dries very quickly and I can apply about 10 coats in 30 minutes. I get very comfortable in a chair and apply finish until my paper towel disintegrates or I get bored, whichever comes first. **NEVER USE CLOTH AROUND A LATHE!!!** If it gets tangled up, it could pull your finger or arm off!!!!!

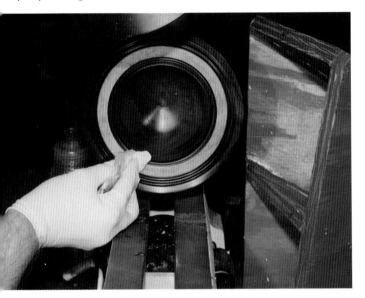

Figure 117. Apply finish with a paper towel. **NEVER USE CLOTH AROUND A LATHE!!!**

Inlace

The inlay material that I used, "Inlace" is a very nice material if you understand its limitations and learn how to work with it. (See Figure 118.) First, it takes a long time to get hard. (That is okay; you probably need to take a break anyway.) You need to work in a well-ventilated area, and probably you should use a chemical respirator also. The biggest problem that I had with it in other projects is that it is quite runny. That was not a problem in this project since the entire inlay area was flat.

Figure 118. Inlace™ is a very nice material if you understand its limitations and learn how to work with it.

However, if you decide to go around the curved surface of the bowl you will need to be prepared to deal with it wanting to run. There are several ways to deal with this. You can use duct tape to help hold the material in place as you rotate the bowl to

add material to another area. Also you can let the material get thicker before you apply the material. (As a dentist I have a hard time forcing myself to do this. In dentistry allowing dental impression material to get thick before you use it is considered bad form.)

A new technique is to add a small amount of "System Three™" (available from Woodcraft Supply) to your mix. This makes the Inlace become thick putty. This putty is supposed to be easy to place and will stay in place well. (I have not used it myself.)

Parting Off

Use your bowl gouge to remove any excess thickness toward the base of the bowl. (See Figure 119.) This will allow you to get better access with your parting tool. Now use your parting tool to cut the bowl free from the glue block. (See Figure 120.) Be sure to have a good grip on the parting tool. Cut toward the tailstock so that you end up with a concave bottom. If you like you can sand the bottom and apply finish. Congratulations, you are finished!! However, if you want to reverse turn the bottom you have a couple more steps to go.

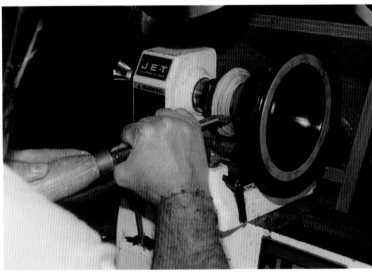

Figure 119. Use your bowl gouge to remove any excess thickness toward the base of the bowl. This will allow you to get better access with your parting tool.

Figure 120. Use your parting tool to cut the bowl free from the glue block. Be sure to have a good grip on the parting tool.

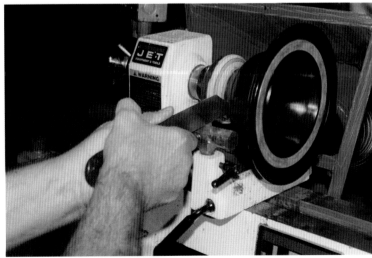

Reverse Turning the Bottom of the Bowl

Reverse turning the bottom of your bowl is very often considered an indication of advanced turning ability. A turned bottom often looks more professional or advanced than a parted off and sanded bottom.

Making a Jam Chuck

Start by mounting your faceplate on a piece of soft scrap wood. I used a piece of scrap 2x10 that was left over from making the staircase in my shop. (See Figure 121.) I marked the center with a straight edge and used a compass to make a circle just a little bigger that the faceplate. Also go ahead and mark the largest circle you can make on the square. Cut the blank round on your band saw.

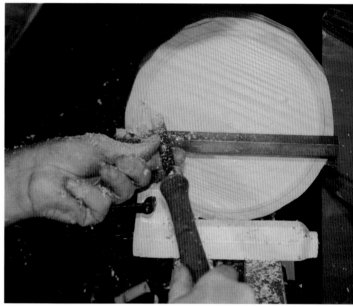

Figure 122. Cut a small "test" rebate into the jam chuck. It should initially be a little too tight on the lid of the bowl. When the fit is "perfect," make the rebate about 1/2 of an inch deep. (A rebate is a small 90 degree step or shoulder cut into the wood.)

Reverse Turning with a Jam Chuck

Insert your bowl into the jam chuck. Bring the tailstock into position and lock. The bowl is now supported at both ends. (See Figure 123.)

Figure 121. Make a jam chuck out of scrap soft wood. This jam chuck is used to reverse turn the bottom of the bowl.

The only real requirement on the screws for the faceplate is that they must be strong enough to hold the wood and not so long that they go through the 2x10. I used the same 5/8-inch screw that I used earlier.

Now mount the faceplate on your lathe. Use your compass to draw a circle of the same diameter as that of the rim of your bowl. If you err, make the error on the side of being a little too small. Use your skew to cut about 1/16 of an inch into the circle. Test fit the rim of the bowl into the recess. Hopefully it is a little too small. Now slightly enlarge the diameter a little bit at a time until the bowl almost fits into the recess or rebate. Now use a square scraper to deepen the rebate to about 1/2 inch. Be careful not to make the diameter larger during this process. (See Figure 122.)

Now very carefully enlarge the diameter of the rebate until the rim of the bowl fits in snugly. Go very slowly and carefully. You need a very accurate fit. If you get it just a little bit too large you can take up some small amount of slack by inserting a paper towel into the rebate.

Figure 123. Insert your bowl into the jam chuck. Bring the tailstock into position and lock. The bowl is now supported at both ends.

Reshape the bottom of the bowl using a very sharp gouge or skew. Cut gently and carefully. This is the place where you want to use a gentle touch.

Use a sharp skew to cut a cove at the bottom of the bowl. (See Figure 124.) This really sets off the bottom of the bowl. Use your skew or small gouge to cut toward the live center. You want the bottom of the bowl concave so that it will still sit flat after doing some minor warping. (See Figure 124.) (Wood is never entirely stable. It will always have slight movement with changes in the moisture content of the air.)

Figure 124. Reshape the bottom of the bowl using a very sharp gouge or skew. Cut gently and carefully. This is the place where you want to use a gentle touch. Use your skew or small gouge to cut toward the live center.

Use duct tape to secure the bowl to the jam chuck. Remove the tailstock. (See Figure 125.) Now very carefully use a sharp scraper or skew to remove the final nub on the bottom of the bowl.

Figure 125. Use a sharp skew to cut a cove at the bottom of the bowl. This really sets off the bottom of the bowl. Use duct tape to secure the bowl to the jam chuck.

Finish the Bottom

Now sand the bottom of the bowl and apply finish. (See Figure 126.) Remove the duct tape and gently remove the bowl from the jam chuck. You are finished!!

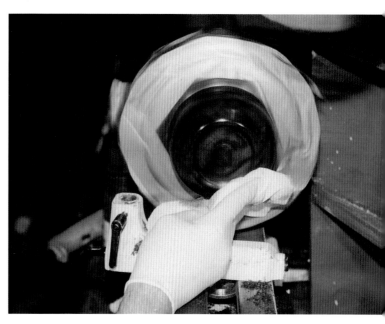

Figure 126. Sand and apply finish to the bottom of the bowl.

Conclusion

Congratulations!! You have just completed an advanced turning project. You have learned several difficult turning procedures that you will use for years to come. In addition you have created a beautiful inlayed bowl that you and your family will enjoy for years to come.

Figures 127a.

Figures 127a-b. The Inlace is a beautiful material to highlight the natural beauty of the walnut.

Figures 127b.

A Beautiful Potpourri Pot

Potpourri pots are very pretty and always have a place of honor in the home. These beautiful pots are a lot of fun to make. They make great gifts and they sell very well at craft fares. Making a potpourri pot is a great learning experience and you will enjoy the end result.

In this exercise you will learn how to turn a square blank round. This is a useful exercise because many turners do not have a band saw. Once the blank is turned round, you can mount it on a faceplate or a 4-jaw chuck. In this exercise we will mount it on a 4-jaw chuck. But you could have mounted it on a faceplate just as easily.

The Potpourri Lid

Potpourri lids are available from Craft Supplies and Woodcraft Supply.

The Turning Blank

We are using dried wood that you can buy from your turning supplier. Choose a hard wood that is very pretty to you. Dried dense wood has several advantages. It is not going to shrink and crack because of drying. Dense wood cuts well and has less tear out than soft wood. Hard dense wood sands well and take a beautiful finish. The disadvantages of dry wood are that it is more expensive because you usually have to buy it and it is hard to cut. I am using 40-year-old air-dried wood in this project. My walnut blank is 4 inches thick. Your blank will probably be 3 inches thick, which is fine.

Square Blank

In this exercise we will be starting with a dry square turning blank. Many turners do not have a band saw to cut their turning blank round. That is OK. In this exercise we will start with a square blank and turn it round.

Start by drawing diagonal lines corner to corner. (See Figure 128.) This finds the center of the blank for you. (In Figure 128, I used a large live center from my big lathe and a rubber hammer. Also note that my face shield and respirator are out and ready to go. You need a shield and some form of air filtration.) Next make a slight indent in both centers. This makes mounting a little easier. This becomes a little more important when you start mounting 40-pound turning blanks. Mount the turning blank between centers. (See Figure 129. Notice the tool holder that sits in the ways of the lathe in photograph 2. Buddy Rose, a wood turning friend, made this for me.) Lock the tailstock in place and lock the live center. Bring the

Figure 128. In this exercise we will start with a square blank and turn it round. Start by drawing diagonal lines corner to corner. This finds the center of the blank for you.

Figure 129. Mount the turning blank between centers. Bring the tool rest into position and check to make sure that the turning blanks rotates without hitting the rest.

tool rest into position and check to make sure that the turning blank rotates without hitting the rest.

Speed

Like all the other projects in this book, we are turning a large object (compared to the size of the lathe). Therefore the speed must be set to the lowest speed, which is 500 RPM. It will remain at this speed for the entire project. Put your face shield on and step to the side of the lathe as you turn it on.

Turning Square To Round

Sharpen your bowl gouge before you start cutting. Turning a square block round is not hard, but it does require you to be patient. As you start out you will be cutting air, except for the brief moment that you cut a small piece of the corner. So you will be hearing and feeling a lot of "**THUMP, THUMP, THUMP, THUMP.**" Go slow and make small cuts. (See Figure 130.) You cannot hurry this part. Point the bowl gouge straight in and use only the small part of the tip of the gouge. Or you may present only a small part of the side of the gouge to the revolving turning blank. (See Figure 131.) Work slowly, taking small bites with the tool. The turning blank will slowly start losing its corners.

Figure 130. Turning a square block round is not hard, but it does require you to be patient. Point your bowl gouge straight into the square and make very small cuts.

Figure 131. You may present a small part of the side of the gouge to the revolving turning blank. Work slowly, taking small bites with the tool. The turning blank will slowly start losing its corners.

As you cut off the corners you will be cutting less and less air and more and more wood. The sound and feel will become more of a "Thump, Thump, Thump..." Continue to make slow, gentle cuts. (See Figure 131.) Eventually you will have more round area than flat spots. You can start making a little bit more aggressive cuts now. As you get almost round you will be getting slightly bigger shavings coming off. (You will never get real big shavings because this is dry wood.) (See Figure 132.) You will now be going "thump, thump, thump."

Continue until the blank is completely round.

Figure 132. As the turning blank becomes round you can switch over to a shear cut with your bowl gouge. Continue until the blank is completely round.

Preparing the Spigot for a 4-Jaw Chuck

Re-arrange your tool rest so that you can square off the tailstock end. Set your calipers to the diameter of your 4-jaw chuck when it is almost (but not quite) closed. (See Figure 133.) Cut your tenon to this diameter. You can use your bowl gouge to do most of the cutting. (See Figure 134.) But do the final shaping with your skew. (See Figure 136.) Use your calipers to make sure that your tenon is the right diameter. (See Figure 135.)

Figure 133. To prepare a spigot for a 4-jaw chuck it is necessary to use calipers to get a good measurement.

Figure 134. Use a bowl gouge to remove the bulk of the wood in making the spigot. The final cuts are made with a skew.

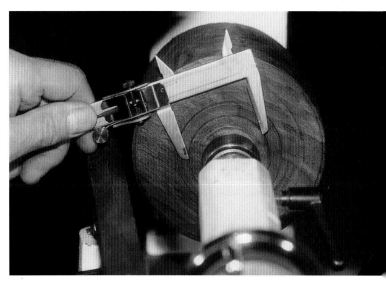

Figure 135. Use your calipers to get the correct diameter of the spigot.

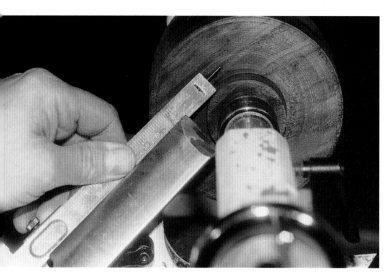

Figure 136. Use your calipers to measure how long to make the spigot. Use your sharp skew to make a nice square shoulder that will fit on the rim of the 4-jaw chuck.

You want the tenon to be very square to the base. Some jaws require that you make a small bead at the lip of your tenon. Look at your jaws to see if you need this little cut to make the jaws fit tight. Be sure that your tenon is short enough so that the tenon does not touch the bottom of the jaws. In this way the turning blank will rest on the shoulder of the jaws and be much more stable and resistant to being dislodged during turning. (See Figure 135. In this photograph I am showing the small ruler sticking out at the end of the calipers. This measurement was set for the depth of my jaws. The skew is what I will use to make the final cut square to the tenon.)

Once you have the tenon the correct size, it is time to take the round turning blank off of the lathe. Use a sharp chisel and mallet to pare off the nub from the tailstock end. (See Figure 137. Normally I would do this on a solid work bench. But this is where I had my camera set up, so this is where I did it this time.)

Figure 137. Use a chisel to remove the small nub that was left from turning between centers.

Mounting to a 4-Jaw Chuck

You can mount your 4-jaw chuck on the lathe and then mount the turning blank. Or you can set the 4-jaw chuck up right on your workbench and put the blank into the 4-jaw chuck. The advantage

to the last technique is that it might be a little easier to make sure that the turning blank is fully seated square in the 4-jaw chuck. Tighten the jaws of the 4-jaw chuck firmly.

Bring the tailstock up and lock it in place. Note that you do not use the center point in the tailstock to tell you how to seat the blank into the 4-jaw chuck. It is possible that at this point the tailstock indentation is no longer in alignment with the square shoulders of the turning blank.

Advance the live center into the turning blank and lock it in place. It is very important to use a tailstock whenever possible. This adds a tremendous amount of safety. It is very difficult (but not impossible) for a piece to fly lose when it is held from both ends.

Rough Shaping the Outside

The turning blank is now held by the 4-jaw chuck (or faceplate) and the live center. Re-true the turning blank with you bowl gouge. (See Figure 138.) Any time you remount your turning on a wood lathe you will lose a little bit of alignment. It is always necessary to go back and re-true the turning.

Figure 138. Mount your 4-jaw chuck and turning blank on the lathe. Make sure that the turning blank is securely seated and that the jaws are very tight.

Start shaping the outside of the pot using your bowl gouge. This is a good time to practice you bevel rubbing technique. Make a slight ridge for your bowl gouge to follow and try to cut all the way up to your 4-jaw chuck. (See Figure 139.) Be careful to not allow your gouge to hit the metal 4-jaw chuck. This quickly ruins the edge of the gouge.

Draw a circle around the turning blank about 3/5 of the way from the bottom. (See Figure 140.) The 3/5– 2/5 proportion is a

Figure 139. Use your bowl gouge to re-true the turning blank.

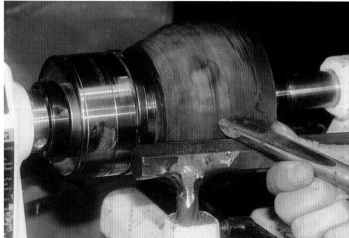

good approximation of the "Golden Rule" guide to proportion. Start rounding from the red line toward the top. Be sure to move you tool rest close to the work area.

Figure 140. Develop the general shape of the pot using your bowl gouge.

Move your tool rest to the top of the turning and flatten the end. (See Figure 141.) Now draw the diameter of the potpourri lid onto the top of the turning. (See Figure 142.) The top of the lid is 3 inches in diameter. In your shaping you must leave enough room for the lid to have a home. The red line at the tailstock end helps you to see how much wood you can remove. Leave at least 1/4-inch space between the lid and the edge. (See Figure 143.) You can cut this down later if you want to.

Figure 141. Flatten the top of the pot with your bowl gouge.

Figure 142. Draw the diameter of the potpourri lid onto the top of the turning.

Figure 143. Leave at least a 1/4-inch space between the lid and the edge. You can cut this down later if you want to.

Continue to refine the shape of the pot. Keeping in mind that this American Indian shape has no straight lines or edges.

Fill Defects

Fill defects with cyano-acrylic glue. (See Figure 144.) If the cracks are very large, add some fine saw dust to the cyano-acrylic glue and push into place with you finger. This gets real messy so put a glove on if you are going to be rubbing your finger in the cyano-acrylic glue. Depending on your type of cyano-acrylic glue, you may or may not need to use an accelerator to make it harden.

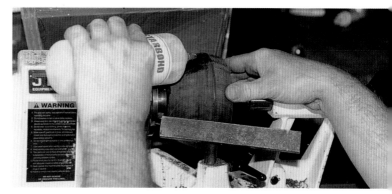

Figure 144. Fill defects with cyano-acrylic glue.

Now go back and put the final touches on the outside shape with your bowl gouge. Cut through and remove any thick cyano-acrylic glue areas. (See Figure 145.)

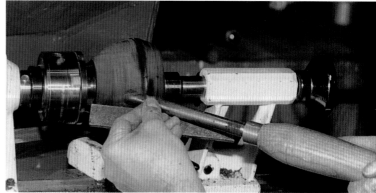

Figure 145. Put the final touches on the outside shape with your bowl gouge. Cut through and remove any thick cyano-acrylic glue areas.

Drill Out the Inside

Mark the bottom of the bowl and how thick you want the floor of the bowl to be. (See Figure 146.) Set the depth gauge (using duct tape) on the drill bit to show how deep to drill into the bowl. (See Figure 146.)

Figure 146. Mark how deep you want the inside of the bowl to be on your drill bit.

Make a slight indentation in the center mark at the tailstock area so that your drill bit has a starting point. Remove the tailstock and drill to the indicated depth. (See Figure 147.) Be sure to back the drill bit out often so that it does not clog up and overheat. Overheating is bad for the drill bit and bad for the wood.

Figure 147. Drill out the inside of the bowl...

Fitting the Lid

Check the circle where the lid goes to make sure it is the correct size. Use your skew to make a sharp cut about 1/16 of an inch deep. Now put your lid into the indentation to make sure it fits correctly. If the fit is correct make the depth about 1/8-inch deep using your sharp skew. (See Figure 148.)

Figure 148. ...and cut a small rebate for the lid to fit into.

Now use a pencil to mark a 1/4-inch wide lip for the lid to sit on. (See Figure 149.)

Figure 149. Use a pencil to mark a 1/4-inch wide lip for the lid to sit on.

The Tool Rest

In your turning you need to be able to get your tool rest close to the area that you are working. To cut the inside of the bowl it is very nice to have a tool rest that will reach up inside the bowl. In this way the tool is supported very close to where you are working. This makes your cutting much easier and gives you a much better finish cut. For this project I made a little curved tool rest that fits nicely inside the bowl. If you would like to have a curved tool rest for small bowls, just contact me. I can custom make you one.

Hollowing the Inside

Use you thin parting tool to make a demarcation cut. (See Figure 150.) I have the tool turned sideways here so that you can see the tool. This will prevent your bowl gouge from kicking back and marring the pot. Now use your bowl gouge to hollow out the inside of the pot. Start by working from the outside toward the center. (See Figure 151.) Having the center drilled out makes this job much easier.

Figure 150. Use a parting tool to cut into the bowl at the edge of the lid lip. This will help prevent kick back of the bowl gouge.

Figure 151. Use your bowl gouge to hollow out the inside of the pot. Cut from the outside in. Later you can learn to cut from the inside out.

Cut a large central cylinder all the way to the depth you measured. Now you can start cutting the pot to the wall thickness that you want.

Place your tool rest as close to the work area as you can. I like to put my tool rest inside the bowl. In this way I get much cleaner and easier cuts. (See Figure 152.) Put your bowl gouge up on its edge and make shaving cuts as you pull out with the gouge. Continue doing this until you have a uniform thin thickness.

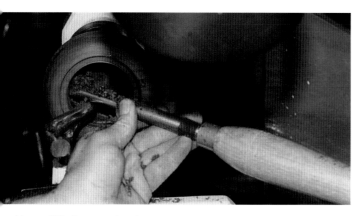

Figure 152. Put your bowl gouge up on its edge and make shaving cuts as you pull from the center out with the gouge. Continue doing this until you have a uniform thin thickness.

Use your round scrapper to make a smooth finish cut on the entire inside. Once again, to make a good cut it is necessary for you to have your tool rest close to the work. (See Figure 153.)

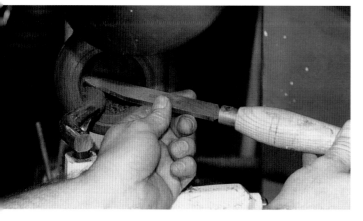

Sanding

It is necessary to control dust and fumes when you are working. The dust from your work can be very dangerous. Figure 154 shows my setup when I am about to start sanding. I have a box fan toward the left blowing dust toward the vacuum box on the right. The box fan has a filter taped to the back of it. (Yes, it is sitting catty-corner inside an empty trashcan.) My vacuum empties outside of my shop. This makes sure that dust is not re-circulated back into my shop.

Figure 154. It is necessary to control dust and fumes when you are working. The dust from your work can be very dangerous. I have a box fan on the left blowing dust toward the vacuum box on the right.

Use rough sandpaper to blend the external lines of the pot. (See Figure 155.) Here I am using about a 60 grit sandpaper to blend all my lines into one contentious form. The photograph does not show it, but a thick stream of sawdust is blowing into the blue vacuum duct.

Figure 155. Use rough sandpaper to blend together the external lines of the pot. Here I am using about a 60 grit sandpaper to blend all my lines into one continuous form. The photograph does not show it, but a thick stream of sawdust is blowing into the blue vacuum duct.

Figure 153. Use your round scrapper to make a smooth finish cut on the entire inside. To make a good cut it is necessary for you to have your tool rest close to the work area.

Applying Finish

Apply your finish while the bowl is still on the lathe. Wet the inside and outside. I use a 50/50 mix of Deft cellulose finish diluted with lacquer thinner. This dries quickly and gives a nice satin finish. Allow each coat to dry about 3 minutes between applications. Use a paper towel to apply the finish and wipe off the excess.

Parting Off

Use your thin parting tool to separate the pot from the lathe. Do not cut straight across, but cut slightly toward the tailstock. This will give you a nice concave bottom. Be sure to have a good grip on the parting tool. When the bowl is just about parted off use the right hand to catch the bowl as the left hand finishes the cut. (See Figure 156.)

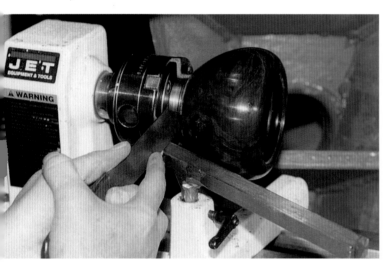

Figure 156. Make an initial cut with the parting tool. Then refine the shape of the bottom of the bowl. Sand and apply finish. Then part the bowl off.

Use a small sharp chisel or knife to cut the nub off the bottom. (See Figure 157.) Be careful to not slip and poke yourself. Sand the bottom. I like to use a foam pad that grips the sandpaper with Velcro™. This is a very quick way to sand the bottom. In a normal sanding situation I would be about 6 inches closer to my vacuum duct. (See Figure 158.)

Apply finish to the bottom and hand rub it in.

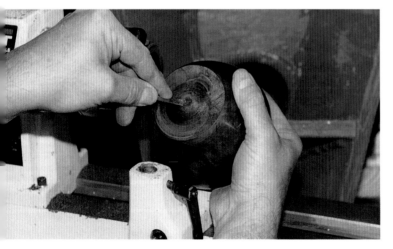

Figure 157. Remove the small nub on the bottom of the bowl with a sharp knife or gouge.

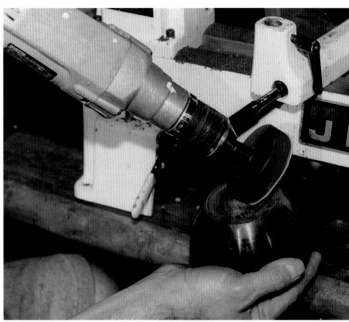

Figure 158. Sand the bottom of the bowl with a foam pad sander. Have it close to a fan or vacuum to control dust.

Conclusion

Making a potpourri pot is a fun project that will teach you some important turning skills. The potpourri pots are beautiful and make nice gifts.

Figure 159. The potpourri pots are beautiful and make nice gifts.

Make a Woven Rim Indian Pot

American Indian pottery has become extremely popular in the last 40 years. Pottery served as an integral part of the lives of all Indian tribes in both function and art. This was true of all Indian tribes from the ancient Hohokam to the present day Hopi. Utility vessels produced centuries ago had forms that met the demands of their times.

This woven rim Indian pot is one of my favorite turning projects. I learned it from Phil Brennion of Chinno Valley, Arizona. If you would like to see more of Phil's work you can visit with him at philb@northlink.com.

American Indian Form

There are usually no sharp lines from the body to the lips of southwest-style vessels. The greatest circumference is reached at just under 3/4 the height of the vessel. The diameter of the rim should be no more that 1/2 to 1/4 of the greatest diameter of the body. The base should be 1/3 the diameter of the rim. These ratios could change for a different type of Southwest vessel and may be exactly reversed.

Selecting and Mounting the Turning Blank

For this project I used a piece of wet Red Bud that was 8 inches long and 5 1/2 inches in diameter. This was wood I collected during the winter of 2001, when we had the worst ice storm in our history. We were without electricity for a week, but I collected some really nice wood. (You can always find something good in every situation.)

Mount the blank between centers. Lock the tailstock in place and tighten the live center. Lock it into place. Place your tool rest and make sure that the turning blank can rotate freely without hitting the tool rest. For this roughing out process I like to use my large tool rest. It allows me to go from one end to the other. (See Figure 160.) Set your speed to the lowest setting, which is 500 RPM.

Figure 160. Mount the blank between centers. Lock the tailstock in place and tighten the live center.

Turning The Blank Round

Sharpen your bowl gouge before starting. Put your face shield on and stand to the side of the lathe as you turn it on. Your lathe should be running smoothly, without any vibration. If the lathe is jumping around, turn it off and make adjustments. The adjustments might include the following: re-centering the wood, shortening the wood, removing projections, or using a different piece of wood. You will be knocking off a lot of bark so you might enjoy having on

a leather glove. (See Figure 161.) Use the tip of your bowl gouge and advance it very slowly straight into the wood. You should be hearing a faint "click, click, click," *not **"Bonk, Bonk, Bonk."*** Slowly remove the bark. If the wood is wet and fairly round, this is a very easy job. But it does take a few minutes.

Figure 161. Use your bowl gouge to remove the bark. Point it straight in and remove a very little bit at a time.

Continue removing bark until all the bark is gone. Reset the tool rest as necessary. Remember life is much easier when you have your tool rest close to the wood. You can make the turning blank smooth and even by presenting the edge of the bowl gouge to the wood and making a shearing cut. This is when the real fun begins. You can get beautiful ribbons to come off the log. (See Figure 162.)

Figure 162. You can use the side of your bowl gouge to make a shear cut once the turning blank has been turned even.

Next move your tool rest to the tailstock end of the lathe. Use your bowl gouge to square up the end of the turning blank. (See Figure 163.) Remember to leave a short tenon of the same diameter as in the center of your faceplate. This will help you center the faceplate on the turning blank.

Figure 163. Use your bowl gouge to square up the end of the turning blank. Remember to leave a short tenon the same diameter as in the center of your faceplate. This will help you center the faceplate on the turning blank.

Mounting the Turning Blank

Take the turning blank off the lathe and mount it, using your faceplate that has 8 holes in it. This is a large piece of wood, so you will need a big screw that goes in the wood at least 1 1/2 inches. (See Figure 164.) Notice the black line on the turning blank. This is how deep the screw goes into the wood. This is good to know so that you do not put the bottom of your bowl in the area where a screw hole lives. It is a good ideal to always take note of how deep the screw goes into your turning blank.

Figure 164. Mount your turning blank to your face plate using big screws that go into the wood at least 1 to 1 1/2 inches.

Turning the Bowl

Attach (screw) the faceplate and turning blank onto the lathe. (See Figure 165.) Draw out what you think will be an attractive looking pot. You will notice on the left of the photograph that my original screw line is present. I have marked off a thick base to give me some "error" freedom. I drew what I thought would be a good initial design. Notice that I have about an inch of excess wood on the tailstock end.

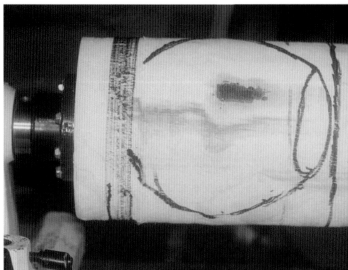

Figure 165. Attach (screw) the faceplate and turning blank onto the lathe. Draw out what you think will be an attractive looking pot.

Use your bowl gouge to cut away excess wood at the tailstock end. (See Figure 166.) This will create a small tenon. (See Figure 167.) Part this tenon away. (See Figure 168.) Turn off the lathe and bring the tailstock into position again. Lock into place.

Figure 166. Use your bowl gouge to cut away excess wood at the tailstock end.

Figure 167. Shortening the turning blank creates a small tenon.

Figure 168. Part the small tenon away with your bowl gouge, skew, or parting tool.

Use your bowl gouge to make initial shaping cuts. You will be cutting away some from the top and the bottom to start creating the correct curves. (See Figure 169.) The black line through the middle is my initial estimate of where the thickest part of the pot will be. Make a long straight cut from the widest part of the pot to the tailstock to make the top of the pot. (See Figure 170.)

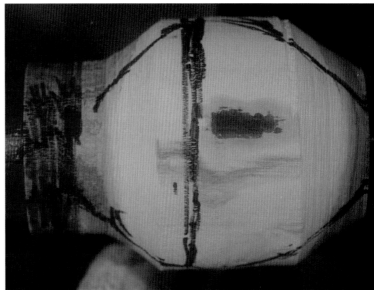

Figure 169. Redraw the shape of the bowl.

Figure 170. Refine the top part of the pot using your bowl gouge.

51

Use your bowl gouge to round in the bottom of the pot. (See Figure 171.) At this stage the turning is still looking "real stubby." That is ok. We will continue to shape it and make it look more delicate.

Next make a straight cut from the large diameter of the bowl toward the tailstock. (See Figure 173.) This is a bevel rubbing cut and gives a pretty nice finish. Notice on Figure 173 that I have drawn a black line about 1/2-inch from the top. I have decided that the pot was this much too long.

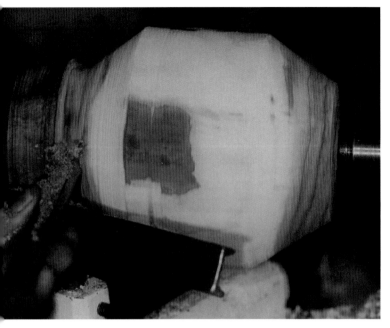

Figure 171. Use your bowl gouge to refine the bottom of the pot. Do not make the bottom very narrow at this time. A large base is necessary to support hollowing out the inside of the pot.

Figure 173. Complete the outside shape of the bowl with a fine bevel rubbing cut.

Redraw your shape lines onto the turning blank. (See Figure 172.) Then use the side of your bowl gouge to round over the bottom, making a shear cut. At this point you should be developing a round bottom on the pot.

In Figure 174 I marked the excess material of the pot in red and parted it off with a bowl gouge.

Figure 172. Use the side edge of you bowl gouge to refine the shape of the bowl.

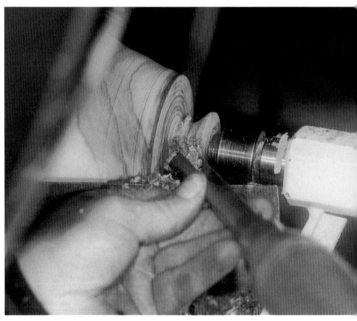

Figure 174. Shorten the top of the pot if you think it is too long.

Now use the side of your bowl gouge to make very fine shear cuts to soften the edges on the top of the pot. (See Figure 175.)

Figure 175. Make very fine shear cuts to the top as finish cuts.

Use the same side shear cut to refine the bottom of the pot. (See Figure 176.) Use the same cut to come all the way around to the middle of the pot. (See Figure 177.)

Figure 176. Make very fine shear cuts to the bottom as finish cuts.

Figure 177. Blend all of the lines together with a very fine shear cut.

Cutting the Rim Rebate

Use your skew to cut a 3/8-inch wide rebate at the rim. A rebate is a small step or shoulder. The rebate should be about 1/8-inch deep. This gives a place for the leather lacing to "live." (See Figure 178.)

This completes the rough shaping of the outside of the pot.

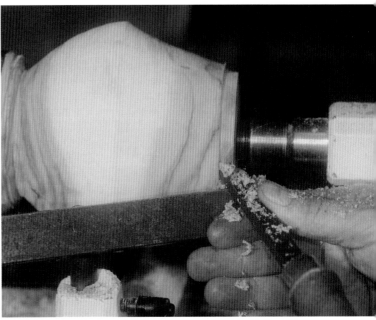

Figure 178. Use your skew to cut a 3/8-inch wide rebate at the rim of the pot. The rebate should be about 1/8 inch deep.

Drilling Out the Inside

Use a piece of tape on your drill bit to mark how deep you want to drill. (See Figure 179.) In the beginning it might be best to leave your bottom a little thick. (It is easy to cut through the bottom while trying to make that bottom perfectly smooth.) Make a little indentation at the tailstock end so that your drill bit will have a starting place. Drill out the inside to the desired depth. (See Figure 180.) Note that you need to take your bit out several times and clean away the shavings. If you go too fast, the drill flutes will clog up and overheat. Then the drill bit will get stuck, and you will have a fine time backing the drill bit out. (Does it sound like I have done this before?)

Figure 179. Mark your drill bit with duct tape to show how deep you need to drill.

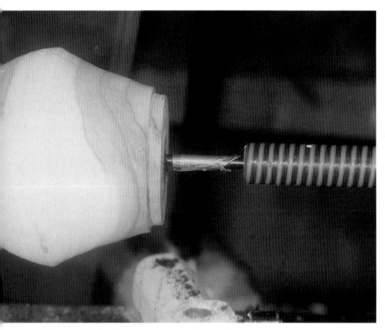

Figure 180. Drill to the correct depth. This will make hollowing the inside much easier.

Mark the Rim Thickness

Use a pencil to mark the rim thickness. (See Figure 181.) Leave this a little thick for now, about 1/4 inch. You can come back later and make it thinner if you want to. Use your thin parting tool to cut the thickness of the rim. (See Figure 182.) This gives you a starting point for your bowl gouge so that you will not get a kick back that will mess up your rim.

Figure 181. Use a pencil to mark how wide the initial wall thickness should be.

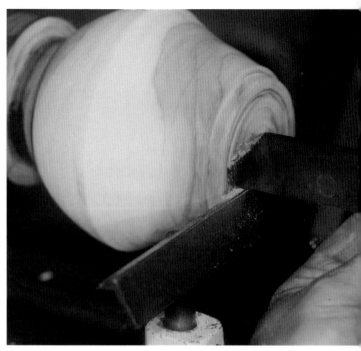

Figure 182. Use a parting tool to start the wall thickness cut. This will help prevent kick back of the bowl gouge.

Cut the Inside of the Pot

Use your bowl gouge to cut out the inside of the pot. Place your tool rest as close as you can to your work area. Make a small starting cut where your parting tool was. Cut toward the center of the bowl. This is a bevel-rubbing cut. Cut slower the closer you get to the center of the bowl. (See Figure 183.) This is necessary because the actual speed of the wood near the center is almost zero.

Figure 183. Use your bowl gouge to hollow out the inside of the pot. Starting out cutting from the outside toward the inside.

You can use the side of your bowl gouge in a shear cut by pulling from the center of the bowl to the outside. (See Figure 184.) This removes a large amount of wood in a hurry. (See Figure 185.) This is also a nice cut because you drag the shavings out with your tool. But be careful not to get a "catch."

Figure 184. You can use the side of your bowl gouge in a shear cut by pulling from the center of the bowl to the outside. This removes a large amount of wood in a hurry.

Figure 185. Using your bowl gouge in a shear cut with a pulling motion can remove a large amount of shavings in a hurry. This is also a nice cut because you drag the shavings out with your tool.

Stop fairly often to check the thickness with your fingers. (See Figure 186.) Your fingers are accurate at this point of the procedure. Later, when you start getting thinner, you may need to start using a thickness caliper. Use your bowl gouge to cut the initial rough thickness of the pot. At this point the bowl should be about 1/2-inch thick.

Finishing the Inside

You can make finish cuts on the inside using the bowl gouge with a shear cut or with a large round scraper. (See Figure 187.) Initially the large round scraper is easier to control. It is very important to get your tool rest very close to the cutting area. This means that the tool rest must fit up inside the bowl. I made an "S" curve tool rest specific for this project.

Figure 187. Refine the inside with a sharp scraper.

With the "S" curve tool rest inside the pot, cut the inside using the tool of your choice. I used a large round scraper that quickly made the inside smooth. (See Figure 188.)

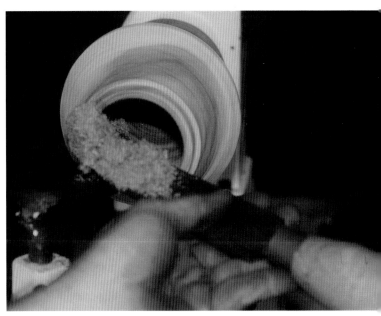

Figure 188. A sharp scraper can remove a large amount of wood in a hurry and leave a very nice surface.

Figure 186. Stop fairly often to check the thickness with your fingers. Your fingers are accurate for this point of the procedure. Later, when you start getting thinner, you may need to start using a thickness caliper.

At this point it is necessary to start using calipers to measure the thickness of the pot. (See Figure 189.) Thin the wall down to about 1/8 to 3/16 thickness. You can leave it a little thicker if you want to. Try not to leave it too thick because the thicker the wet wood is, the more likely it is to crack when it dries. (I know that sounds backwards, but it is true. The pot has a better chance of not breaking if you make it thin with an even thickness.)

Figure 189. Use your calipers to check the thickness as the pot starts to get thin.

Achieving Final Thickness

Final thickness is achieved very carefully with fine finishing cuts. The tool rest must be very close to the area where you are working. Final thickness is achieved at the rim and you slowly work toward the base. Once you have final thickness of the middle **you cannot** go back out to the rim and re-cut. And once you have final thickness of the base **you cannot** go back out to the rim or to the middle. This is especially true of large platters where you will blow up the platter if you go back to the outside rim. (So get used to good turning habits.) Complete the top of the bowl and then carry the same measurement in to the bottom.

Refining the Bottom

You can now refine the bottom of the pot some more. (See Figure 190.) The final refinement will come only after you start making your parting cut. Use your bowl gouge or your skew to round over the edges in the bowl. There should be no sharp edges. (See Figure 191.)

Figure 190. Finish refining the shape of the bottom now that the inside is finished.

Figure 191. Blend all of the lines together with a smooth shear cut.

Sanding

Sanding for this project is a shaping tool. Use course sandpaper (about 80 grit) to blend the curves of the pot. (See Figure 192.) Take out all straight lines and all cut imperfections. Then sand all the way through 400 grit sandpaper. (I would go to 800, but my 600 and 800 sandpapers are black and mar light colored woods.) Sand the inside of the pot at this time also.

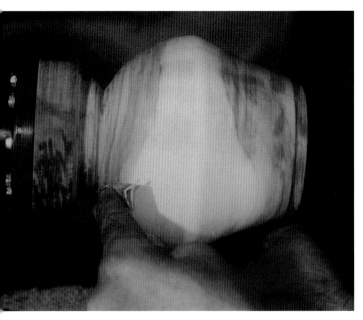

Figure 192. Use coarse sandpaper to eliminate any angles or blemishes. Sand all the way to 400 grit.

Be sure to have a good dust control system going. This could be a fan to your back and an open window or a vacuum system to pick up the dust. The blue box in my photographs is a dust collection hood that I made.

Apply Finish

Apply finish inside and out. Use a paper towel to apply finish. (See Figure 193.) Never use cloth. If the cloth catches it could pull your finger off or, on a bigger lathe, pull your arm off. Get used to good lathe work habits. You might work on a big lathe someday that has a 5 HP motor. I use a 50/50 mixture of Deft cellulose finish diluted with lacquer thinner. It is fast drying and gives a nice satin finish. If you want a high gloss you can spray it later when it is off the lathe. High gloss finishes are hard to photograph so I do very few high gloss finishes.

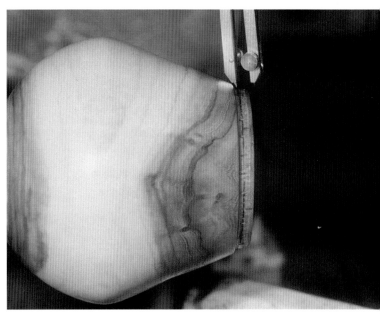

Figure 194. Use a compass to make 3/8-inch divisions around the rim. To make the holes all line up straight make a line that goes around the rim.

Making Holes in the Rim

It is necessary to drill evenly spaced holes around the rim so that we can do the lacing. Use a compass to make 3/8-inch divisions around the rim. (See Figure 194.) To make the holes all line up straight make a line that goes around the rim. Be sure to leave enough room toward the edge so that your drill bit does not break through. You may have to adjust the spacing on the last three holes to make them come out evenly spaced.

Make an initial pilot hole with a 1/8-inch bit. Then go back and enlarge the hole with a 3/16-inch bit. (See Figure 195.) Be careful! The wood is delicate now. Angle the drill bit toward the base of the bowl a little bit. This will give you a little bit more wood to go through.

Lightly sand the rim and holes to take off any wood burs ... again, carefully!

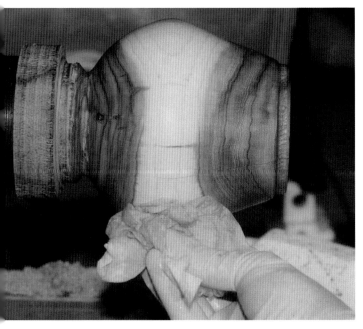

Figure 193. Apply finish inside and out while the pot is still on the lathe. **Never use cloth around a lathe, always use paper towels.**

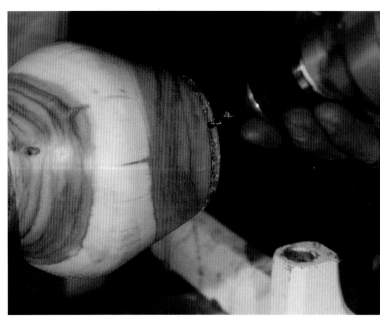

Figure 195. Use your electric drill to make an initial pilot hole with a 1/8-inch bit. Then go back and enlarge the hole with a 3/16-inch bit.

Final Bottom Shaping

Use your thin parting tool to make the parting cut. Cut about half way in. (See Figure 196.) Use your skew to do the final rounding of the bottom of the bowl. (See Figure 197.) Sand again and blend the surfaces together using sandpaper. Reapply finish. (See Figure 198.)

Parting Off

Use your thin parting tool to part the pot off. Trim the nub off with a sharp knife or chisel. Then sand the bottom. I like to use a foam pad that has hook and loop sandpaper on it. This is a very fast and easy way to finish the bottom. (See Figure 199.) Apply finish to the bottom of the bowl and rub in by hand.

Figure 196. Use your thin parting tool to make the parting cut. Cut about half way in.

Figure 199. Sand the bottom of the pot. Foam pads with hook and loop sandpaper are terrific.

Reinforcing the Rim Holes

Place some paper towels or some other type of protection over your work area. Then apply cyano-acrylic glue to the rim and the holes. (See Figure 200.) Hold the bowl upside down so that the glue does not run into the bowl. This will reinforce the rim for the lacing process.

Figure 197. Use your skew to do the final rounding of the bottom of the bowl. Sand again and blend the surfaces together using sandpaper.

Figure 200. Apply cyano-acrylic glue to the holes to reinforce them. Tilt the pot upside down so that the glue does not run into the pot.

Figure 198. Re-apply finish to the outside of the pot.

Leather Lacing

Lacing with leather is a lot of fun and can add a lot of beauty to your turnings. Leather supplies are available from most craft supply stores. The supplies that you need are quite limited. First you need to buy some leather lacing and a couple of split needles. (See Figure 201.) You might also want to buy a few feathers and hollow beads to finish off the project.

Figure 201. The set up for lacing requires only a split needle and leather lacing.

Start off by estimating how much lace you will need. I use 16 times the circumference. So I run a length of lace around the rim. I them double this and double it again. Then double it again. This gives me a length 16 times the circumference and it is usually just about the correct length. If there is an error I am on the long side. I really do not like to do splices so I would rather be long.

Use a pair of scissors to make a point on the end of the leather that will fit up in the eye of the split needle. (See Figure 202.) You can also use a razor blade to feather the leather down to a thin edge so that it fits into the needle easier. Now spread the tail of the needle and insert the leather between the two blades. A barb on one of the blades will hook and hold the leather.

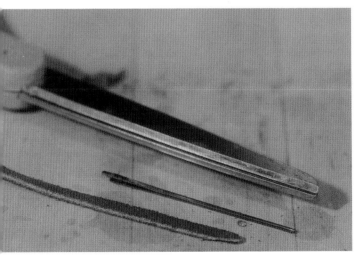

Figure 202. Use your scissors to cut a point on the lacing.

Now come through hole No. 1 from the inside of the pot. Leave enough leather tail for it to hang down in front of the pot. (See Figure 203.) **Throughout this entire lacing, the needle will always come from the inside of the pot to the outside.**

Figure 203. Go through hole #1 from the inside to the outside. Leave a tail long enough to reach the table top.

Now go forward to hole No. 5, move to the inside, and run the needle through hole No. 5. Then insert the needle back under the leather to go back to hole No. 2. (See Figure 204.)

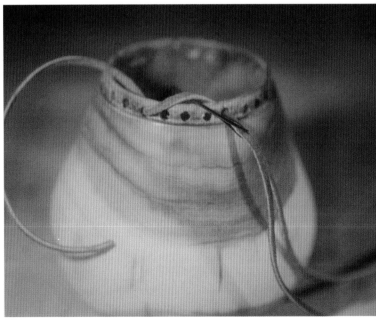

Figure 204. Go forward to the 5th hole. Go to the inside of the pot and push the needle and lace through from the inside to the outside. Then loop the needle back under the lace on the top of the rim.

Now put the needle through hole No. 2 and pull it through. (See Figure 205.)

Now go forward a count of 5, which puts you at hole No. 6. You will loop over to the inside of the pot and come through hole No. 6 from the inside.

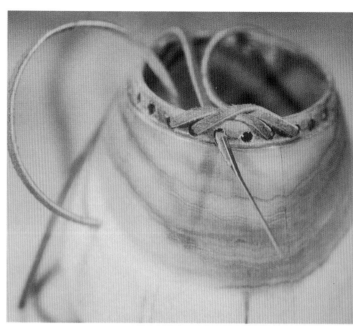

Figure 207. Go back 4 holes to hole #3. Run the needle from the inside to the outside.

Figure 205. Go back 4 holes to hole #2. Put the needle on the inside and run the needle and lace through from the inside to the outside.

Go back a count of 4 so that you come out hole No.3 this time. (See Figure 207.)

Going forward on the outside you always advance 5 holes and going back on the inside you always go back 4. In this way you work yourself around the pot.

This time as you go forward you have to cross 2 pieces of leather. Go under the first and over the second. (See Figure 208.)

When you get to this stage all of the following times there will be 3 pieces of leather to cross over. Go over the first and third and under the middle. This will give you a basket weave pattern.

Next double back underneath the leather that just went to hole No. 6. (See Figure 206.)

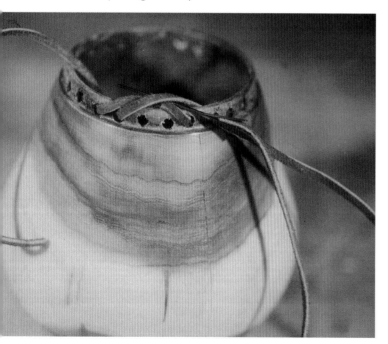

Figure 206. From hole #2 go forward 5 holes to hole #6. (You always go forward 5 holes and back 4 holes.) Go to the inside of the pot and push the needle and lace through to the outside. Loop the needle and lace back under the lace at the top of the rim.

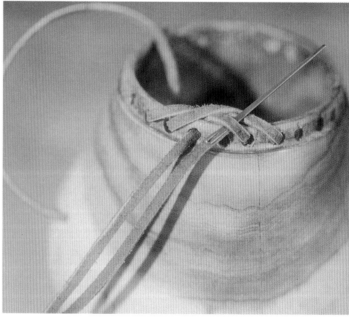

Figure 208. Advance forward with your needle and lace the standard 5 holes. As you go forward it is necessary for you to loop under the first cross lace and over the second cross lace.

Now go over to the inside of the pot and come out the next hole. (See Figure 209.) Then double back under the leather that just went over the rim. (See Figure 210.) Go back 4 holes and come through the next hole. This time as you go forward there will be 3 strips of leather to cross. Go over the first and third and under the middle. (See Figure 211.)

Now go to the inside of the pot and come out the next hole. Then double back under the leather that just came over. (See Figure 212.) Go back 4 holes as before. And continue to repeat.

Figure 211. Push the lace and needle through hole #4 from the inside to the outside. This time there will be three cross lacings. From now on always cross over the first and third and under the 2nd cross lacing.

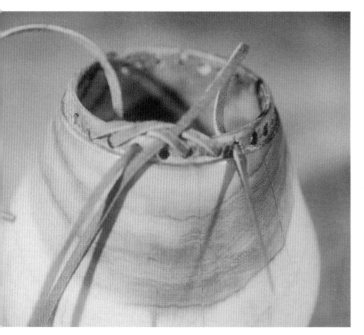

Figure 209. Go to the inside and push your needle and lace through from the inside to the outside of hole #8.

Figure 212. Advance forward to the 5th hole which is now hole #9. Go through from the inside to the outside and loop back under the lace at the top of the rim. Continue this process until finished.

Figure 210. Loop the needle back under the lace at the top of the rim and go back 4 holes to hole #4.

Rules For Lacing

1. Use a length of lacing that is 16 times to circumference of the lid.

2. Going forward on the outside you always advance 5 holes and going back on the inside you always go back 4. In this way you work yourself around the pot.

3. The needle always goes through the hole from the inside toward the outside.

4. When the needle has just gone through the 5th (or forward hole) it immediately ducks back under the lacing that just when through the hole.

5. When going forward through the number one hole (or back hole) skip over the first cross lacing, go under the second cross lacing, and go over the 3rd cross lacing.

Tying Off and Finishing

Once you have gone all the way around the rim with the lacing it is necessary to finish off the leather ends. Thread both ends so that they go under the weave and come out the bottom of the weave beside each other.

You can now cut both pieces of leather at an angle so that the ends are about 1/2- to 1/4-inch off the table. You might quit at this point.

I like to add beads and feathers to the ends of my leather lacing. You can buy beads and feathers from your craft supply store.

Conclusion

Turning and weaving a leather rim on your Indian pot is a lot of fun and makes a beautiful project. You get to learn a lot of turning techniques while having a lot of fun. This is one of the projects that I enjoy the most. It may be because I get so many compliments on the bowls.

Figure 213. You can add beads and feathers to highlight the beauty of the Indian pot.

Turn a Stone Jar

Turning different soft stones, like soapstone and alabaster, can give you some beautiful turning results. Some of my most beautiful turnings are done in stone. You will be able to make a beautiful translucent rock jar that looks like it belongs in a fine arts museum. Stone has some beautiful characteristics. Unlike wood, it does not need to be dried and it does not warp during turning or after the turning process. It will not crack as a result of the drying process. (Many turners will fall in love with stone for this last reason.) The colors of different stones are rich, beautiful, and translucent.

Okay, so what is the down side to turning stone? Well, there are a couple problems. First, turning stone is very dusty. You need to be very careful to use good lung protection and to have a good dust filtration system. Second, you will not be able to cut the fine detail into stone that you can in wood. So, do not start out trying to cut small coves and beads. Strive to cut gentle curves.

The turning techniques are very similar to turning wood. You will be using the same tools that you use for cutting wood. In tuning stone you be doing mostly scraping cuts. Re-sharpen after just a few minutes of cutting.

Material

The world is full of rock, so you are likely to be able to find some not too far from home. However, if you have never looked for it before, you might not know how close it is to you. Many of the turning supply stores handle different types of stone. Also, art supply stores handle it for carvers. When I started turning stone, I found two different towns less than one hundred miles from me that used alabaster to make sheet rock.

Getting Started

Use only good stone. That is the same rule for turning wood. In turning stone it means that you look for fracture lines that are likely to make the turning break. If you do have a small fracture line you might be able to save the rock by reinforcing the flawed stone with cyano-acrylic glue or Weld Bond™ (poly-vinyl acetate sold by Ace Hardware). But for starting off it would be better if you had flawless rock.

Study your rock to see where you should cut to get the best pieces from the rock. Make some practice lines on the rock to make sure you choose the best areas to cut. Then draw a circle on the rock with your compass. (See Figure 214.)

Sawing

Use your band saw to cut your rock blank round. This seems a little weird the first time you cut rock. But if you are cutting soft rock, you will not damage your saw or blade. (See Figure 215.) To make sure that the rock is soft, scratch it with a pocketknife. It should scratch easily. Soapstone cuts as easily as soft wood. Alabaster is harder and cuts a little bit slower. Use regular safety precautions when cutting but also be careful of the dust. And, of course, be sure to use eye protection.

Figure 215. Use your band saw to cut the stone round.

Mounting To A Faceplate

Mount a piece of wood onto your faceplate. I used a piece of plywood that was left over from the woven rim pot in this book. Use a 5-minute quick set epoxy. (See Figure 216.) Mix an ample amount and place onto both surfaces. Place a ring of duct tape around the glue joint to keep the glue from running. (See Figure 217.) Place a small amount of glue on the top and place a small piece of plywood over the glue. The plywood on the top is for the live center to go into. Plywood will sometimes come apart when used for heavy work. I now try to use a good hardwood, like maple, for all of my faceplate mountings. (See Figure 217.)

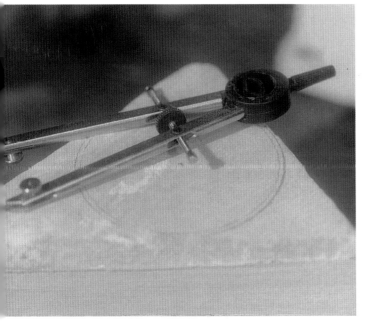

Figure 214. Use your band saw to cut a flat surface on your stone. Then draw the largest circle that you can with your compass.

Figure 216. Use epoxy cement to glue the rock to a plywood base.

Figure 217. Put a piece of duct tape around the epoxy to keep from making a mess. Glue a small piece of plywood to the top of the rock. This will give your live center a place to rest. If you put the live center into rock you will fracture it.

Important question!!! How long does it take for 5-minute epoxy to set?

Duuhh? Actually, it is not such a dumb question. Five-minute epoxy starts to firm up in 5 minutes. In 90 minutes it has an initial set. *In 3 hours it is ready to go!!!* So put your project aside and go do something else for 3 hours or the rest of the night.

Turning Round

Set the lathe speed to its slowest speed, 500 RPM. Put you faceplate and turning stone onto the lathe. Put the tailstock into position and lock. Advance the live center and lock. (See Figure 218.) Place your tool rest and make sure it rotates with out hitting. Put your face shield and respirator on. Put your box fan behind you to blow the dust away from you. Step to the side of the lathe and turn it on.

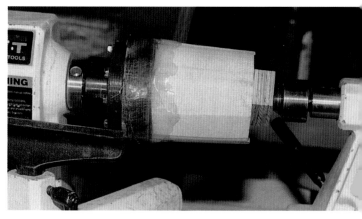

Figure 218. Mount your faceplate and rock turning blank onto the lathe. Position and lock the live center.

Use the small point of your gouge to slowly turn the rock blank round. Go slow and take very small bites of the turning. Work the entire length of the turning. When the turning blank is almost round use the side of your bowl gouge to do a shear-scraping cut. This will produce a smooth flat surface. (See Figure 219.) This creates a nice smooth rock cylinder.

Figure 219. Turn the rock blank round with our regular bowl gouge.

Use a pencil or marking pen to draw a nice pattern onto the cylinder. Use your bowl gouge to slowly start cutting the grooves into the blank. (See Figure 220.) This will make a lot of dust.

Figure 220. Use the tip of your bowl gouge to start shaping the bowl.

Safety Note

In all of these procedures I am wearing a respirator and face shield. In addition I have a fan to my back blowing the dust toward the blue vacuum manifold. (See Figure 220.)

External Shape

Use your bowl gouge, scraper, or your skew to shape the outside of the jar. Any sharp scraping tool will work fine. (See Figure 221.) Refine the shape and create a smooth pleasant looking form.

Figure 221. Use a very fine shear cut and a soft touch to cut the stone.

Drilling The Inside

Mark how deep you want the floor of the jar to be. (See Figure 222.) Then set your drill bit to that distance. In this situation I decided to use a Forstner bit in a Jacob's chuck. This is a very gentle way to drill out a large amount of material. Position the drill bit and slowly advance it into the jar. (See Figure 223.) Notice the very fine dust. Drill all the way to the desired depth.

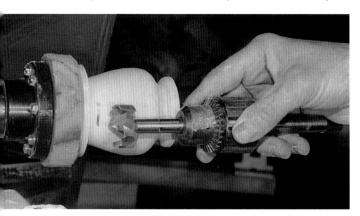

Figure 222. Mark the depth that you want your Forstner™ bit to drill to.

Figure 223. Drill out the central core with the Forstner bit. This is a very fast and easy way to remove a large amount of stone.

Hollowing the Inside

Remove your tailstock and set it aside. Use a scraper to hollow the entire inside. The round nose scraper works very well for this job. (See Figure 224.) Work from the rim toward the base. Make the rim about 1/4 of an inch thick. Slowly work this thickness all the way toward the base. Initially you can use your fingers as a thickness gauge. As you get deeper you might need to use thickness calipers. Position your tool rest as close to the area as you can to get a smooth cut. This material cuts so nice that you may not have to have the tool rest inside the jar to make a good cut.

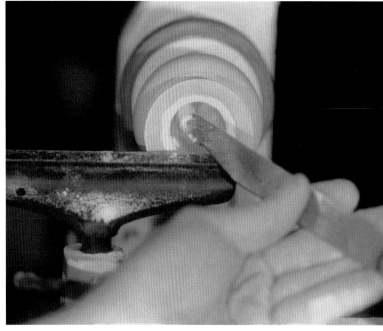

Figure 224. Hollow the inside of the jar with a sharp scraper. This stone cuts so easily that it is not necessary for you to put your tool rest inside the jar.

Finishing the Inside and Outside

Use 120 grit sandpaper to do the final shaping. Blend all curves with this sandpaper. Use this sandpaper to smooth out rough spots on the inside of the jar. Sand all the way through 400 to 800 grit sandpaper. (See Figure 225.)

Figure 225. Sand the stone jaw with fine sandpaper.

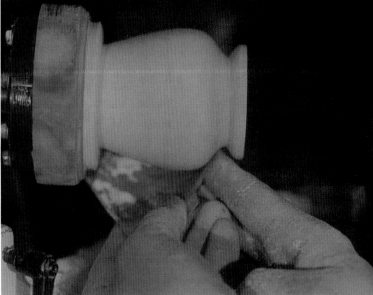

Now use your sharp skew to thin down the base of the jar. (See Figure 226.) Up until this time the base was left large so that there would be a large and strong glue joint. Now that everything is complete, except the bottom, it is time to make this area small.

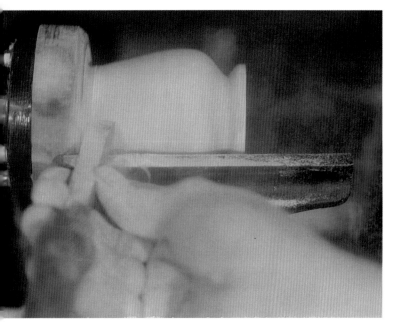

Figure 226. Refine the bottom shape of the jar. Sand again.

Finishing

If you want to use wax, put some wax on your finger and spread it over the entire surface of the jar, inside and out. Use a paper towel to buff the jar. This will produce a nice satin finish.

Wax may darken the stone jar. You may not want it to darken. In this case, a cellulose finish is very nice and very quick to apply. I use my regular mix of Deft cellulose finish and lacquer thinner mixed 50/50. Wet a paper towel and apply to the jar. Turn the lathe on and buff it off with a dry paper towel. **Never use cloth around a lathe.**

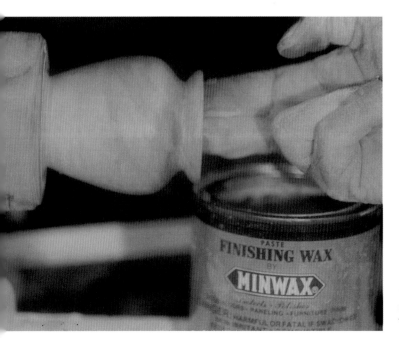

Figure 227. Apply lacquer finish or paste wax. The paste floor wax will make the stone turn a little darker. If you do not want the stone to turn darker use a lacquer finish diluted 50/50 with lacquer thinner.

Parting Off

Use your thin parting tool to cut the jar off the turning waste block. Be careful because rock jars do not bounce well. Sand and finish the bottom by hand. This will only take a few minutes.

Conclusion

Turning stone is fun and the results are beautiful. I think you will have a lot of fun with this project. You should get a lot of compliments from your stone turnings. I have had many people tell me that the stone turnings are some of my best work. People are very impressed with stone turning. Probably because it seems that turning stone should be very difficult.

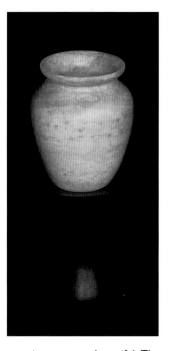

Figure 228. Stone turnings are very beautiful. The only real disadvantage is the dust that the turning creates.

Make a Hawaiian Bowl
A Lesson in Wood Stabilization

I learned how to make this project from Kelly Dunn, who lives in Hawaii. Kelly has made a good living making beautiful bowls from North Folk Island pine. Kelly roughs out the pine and coats the outside with greenwood sealer until dry. Kelly says, "However, a piece can be done green start to finish also. I just rough it out. Let it dry it and then re-turn it."

The pine is a beautiful but soft wood. To keep some wood from splitting, a stabilization process can be useful. Fellow Hawaiian Ron Kent stabilizes his pine by soaking the wood in a detergent soap. Some turners have found that the lubricant WD-40 works very well for stabilizing wood. I decided to stabilize my bowl using a commercial product called Pentacryl™.

Pentacryl was originally developed for the museum industry to stabilize artifacts that were brought up from river bottoms or from the ocean. When word got out how good it was, wood turners started using it. If you are having trouble with your turnings cracking, then you might want to try stabilizing your green turnings.

Choose a wood that is both beautiful and one that has been prone to cracking with you. In this case, I got Kelly to send me some North Fork Island pine. You might try using a fruitwood that has given you trouble. Pentacryl works best on wet wood. Usually bowls that are no thicker than one inch require an over night soaking in Pentacryl. Some woods with high tannin content will darken. This is usually a surface darkening and can be removed with sanding or re-turning.

This is an easy turning, so if it does crack you have not lost too much time. But if it does work for you, you will be able to use woods that you previously rejected because they cracked on you. An aide to preventing cracking is to have evenly thin turnings. A thick or uneven turning is more likely to crack.

Getting Started

Mount your wood between centers and square off one end. (See Figure 229.) You can use either a faceplate or 4-jaw chuck for this project. If you use a 4-jaw chuck, make sure that your spigot is the correct size and do not over tighten the 4-jaw chuck. (See Figure 230.) Over tightening the jaws will cause the spigot to deform. If you dislodge the wood and have to re-chuck the wood, it will never go back to place correctly.

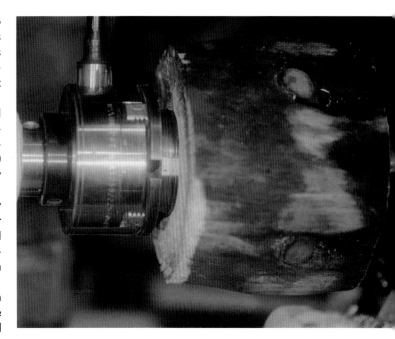

Figure 230. Mount your 4-jaw chuck and the turning blank. Tighten the jaws with that blank securely seated against the jaws of the chuck.

Draw the general shape of the bowl onto the turning blank. (See Figure 231.) This will help you shape the bowl. Sharpen your bowl gouge. Use your bowl gouge to shape the outside of the bowl. (See Figure 232.) This is soft and wet wood, which lets you make beautiful shavings. After you have done some initial shaping, re-draw the shape on the turning blank. (See Layout 233.)

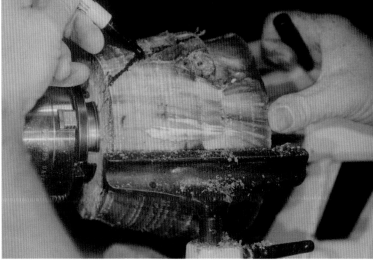

Figure 231. Rough turn the blank and then draw the general shape that you want to cut.

Figure 229. Mount your turning blank between centers. Turn the tailstock end to either accept a faceplate or make a spigot for your 4-jaw chuck.

Figure 232. Use your bowl gouge to shape your bowl.

Cutting the Inside

Mark where you want the bottom of the bowl to be. (See Figure 233.) Set the depth of your drill bit to this mark. (See Figure 234.) Drill out the inside. You can use a narrow drill bit or you can use a wider diameter Forstner bit. Use whatever you have.

Use your bowl gouge to rough out the inside of the bowl. (See Figure 235.) Reduce the wall thickness to an even 1/4 of an inch. Position your tool rest as close as you can to your work area. Then use the side of your bowl gouge in a shear scraping cut or your scraper to make your final finish cuts. (See Figure 236.) Here I am using the inside wing of the "Wish Bone" tool rest. Use your fingers or a thickness calipers to make sure that you have an even thickness. (See Figure 237.)

Figure 233. Redraw the shape as you remove more and more wood.

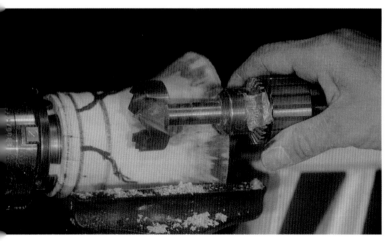

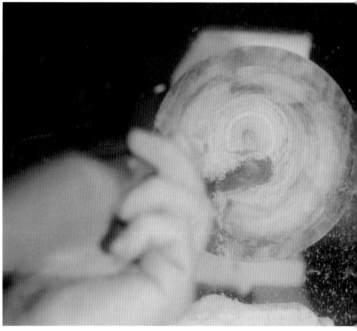

Figure 235. Hollow out the inside with your bowl gouge. Here I am using my "Wish Bone" tool rest so that I can keep my tool rest very close to the tip of my gouge.

Figure 236. Refine the inside shape of the bowl with a large scraper. Here you can get a better look at the "Wish Bone" tool rest.

Figure 234. Set the depth for your Forstner bit and drill out the central core.

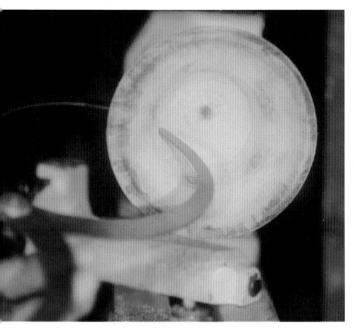

Figure 237. Use your thickness calipers to make sure that the bowl is of an even thickness from top to bottom.

Shaping the Bottom

Use your skew and bowl gouges the shape the foot of the bowl. (See Figures 239-240.) Try to create a small delicate foot. Sand the inside and outside of the bowl. (See Figure 241.) Use your thin parting tool to cut the bowl off. (See Figure 242.)

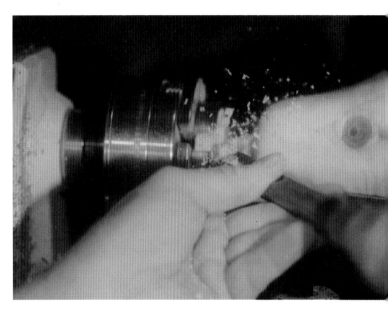

Figure 239. Refine the bottom of the bowl with a bowl gouge.

Refining the Outside Shape

Re-sharpen your bowl gouge. Position your tool rest close to your turning and make a shear cut on the outside. Use this cut to blend all of the curves together. This cut should produce extremely fine shavings. (See Figure 238.) Here I am using the outside wing of the "Wish Bone" tool rest.

Figure 238. Sand the inside then fine tune the outside rim of the bowl.

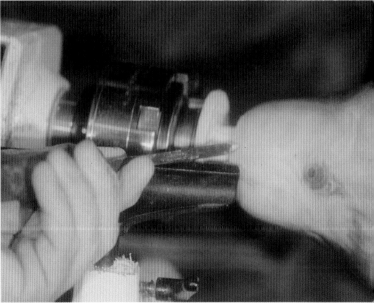

Figure 240. Use your skew to do final shaping on the bottom.

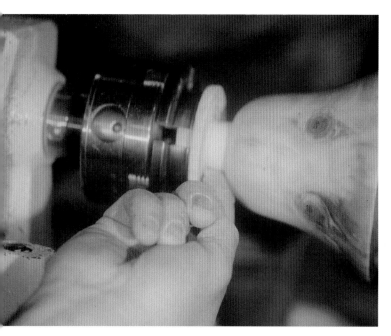

Figure 241. Sand the entire bowl carefully.

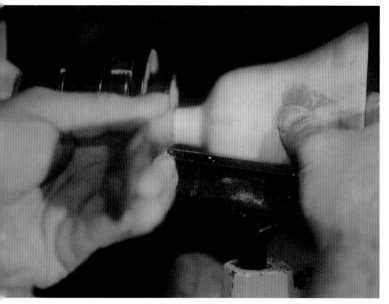

Figure 242. Part the bowl off with a thin parting tool. Sand the bottom.

Stabilizing the Wood

Many turnings will crack when they dry. Stabilizing with a product like Pentacryl will prevent most woods from cracking or splitting. (The manufacturer told me that it would prevent 99 percent of all wood from cracking.) I do not think it is quite that good, but it will stop some cracking and turning headaches.

Soak your thin turning in Pentacryl overnight. I intentionally wanted to cause the sapwood to darken, so I soaked the bowl for 2 days to cause darkening at the rim. Woods that do not have tannic acid in them will not darken.

Drying

Remove the treated bowl and dry with a paper towel. Set the bowl away in a cool, dry place for about 3 weeks. Cool drying is best. Normal drying time of Pentacryl treated wood is 3/4 the time for untreated wood. So, if you spent one year drying a one-inch thick bowl, you would spend 8 months drying a Pentacryl treated bowl. Since your bowl is very thin, it should dry in 3 to 6 weeks depending on the moisture content of your shop.

Pentacryl stabilizes and displaces some of the water. Some of the water it emulsifies. This water has to be slowly dried away as the solvent of the Pentacryl evaporates. It is best if this is a slow process. You can use a moisture meter to check for dryness or you can weigh the bowl to see if it is dry. I have a nice moisture meter, but never use it. Once the bowl has stayed the same weight for a week you can feel comfortable that it is as dry as it is going to get in your area.

Final Finish

When the bowl has completely dried you are ready to apply your finish. You might want to lightly re-sand. Apply your favorite finish.

Conclusion

Stabilizing your green turnings can be a very useful technique to prevent wet turnings from cracking as they dry. This will allow you to use many woods that were previously unusable because they cracked too much.

Ornamental Bird House
Developing a Fine Touch

Professional woodturner Bob Rosand has made a good living making Christmas ornaments. But on January 1, the market for Christmas ornaments became a little slow each year. Bob decided to come up with an ornament that he could make and sell all year long. One of my favorite ornaments that he came up with is the Ornamental Bird House.

This is a beautiful and delicate multi-piece turning. There are 6 separate pieces to this project. All of the pieces are quite small and delicate. Learning to turn this project will indicate that you have developed a lot of turning skill. I have intentionally left it for last. By this time you have developed enough skills that you can attempt this project with a bit of confidence.

The 6 pieces to the birdhouse are: house body, house roof, house floor, roof finial, floor finial, and the perch.

Wood to Use

All of these pieces will be made from pieces of scrap wood that are lying around your shop. Look around your shop and pick up all the pretty pieces of off-cuts that you have. You do save them don't you?

4-Jaw Chuck

This project will be much easier if you have a 4-jaw chuck. However, you can make this project using your faceplate and jam chucks. It will just take a little bit longer.

Making the House Body

Mount a piece of hard, dense wood in your 4-jaw chuck. The body of the house should be about 2 1/4 inches long. Turn the cylinder down to about 2 1/2 inches in diameter. (See Figure 243.) Now use a 1 5/8-inch Forstner bit to drill out the center of the birdhouse. (See Figure 244.) If you do not have a large bit you can use a small bit and then widen the hole with a flat scraper. Use your skew to make sure that the sides of the house are straight and have an even thickness. Reduce the thickness of the wall to about 3/16 to 1/4-inch thick. (See Figure 245.) Sand and apply finish to the body of the birdhouse. (See Figure 246.) Use your thin parting tool to part off the birdhouse from the lathe. (See Figure 247.) Hold the body of the house loosely in your right hand as the left hand makes the cut. In this way you can catch the body when it comes loose.

Figure 243. To make the house body, mount a piece of hard dense wood in your 4-jaw chuck. The body of the house should be about 2 1/4 inches long.

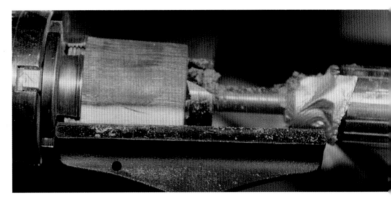

Figure 244. Turn the cylinder down to about 2 1/2 inches in diameter. Now use a 1 5/8-inch Forstner bit to drill out the center of the birdhouse.

Figure 245. Reduce the thickness of the wall to about 3/16 to 1/4-inch thick.

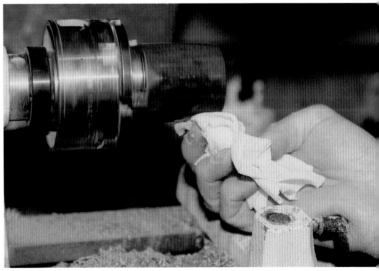

Figure 246. Sand and apply finish to the body of the birdhouse.

Figure 247. Use your thin parting tool to part off the birdhouse from the lathe. Hold the body of the house loosely in your right hand as the left hand makes the cut. In this way you can catch the body when it comes loose.

Drilling the Door and Perch Holes

If you start with square stock, you can drill the holes while the stock is still square. Since I usually start with round scrap wood, I end up drilling through round stock.

Make a round turning support from a piece of scrap 2x4. The support should be about 12 inches long. Tilt the blade on your table saw to 45 degrees. Mark a centerline that goes down the length of the 2x4. Set the fence of the saw so that the cut will be about 1/4-inch from the center. Set the saw blade so that it is about 1/2-inch above the table. Make a cut along the length of the 2x4. Then reverse it end for end and make another cut. This should remove the center of the 2x4 and leave a "V" cut. (See Figure 248.)

Drill a 5/8-inch hole in the middle top third of the house for the door. (See Figure 248.) Then drill a 1/16-inch hole in the middle half of the house for the perch below the door

Figure 248. Drill the door and perch holes.

Making the Floor

Mount a new piece of wood in your 4-jaw chuck. Make it flat at the tailstock end. Turn the piece round. Reduce the diameter to a little larger than 2 inches. Use your calipers to measure the inside thickness of the house floor. Cut a short tenon that will fit into the floor of the house. (See Figure 249.) The floor should fit into the bottom of the house easily without any slop. (See Figure 250.) It cannot fit tight. A tight fit will split the house.

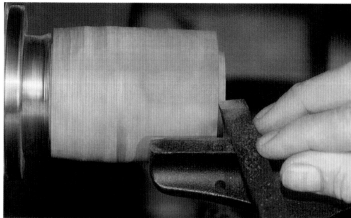

Figure 249. Make a short tenon to fit inside the floor of the house.

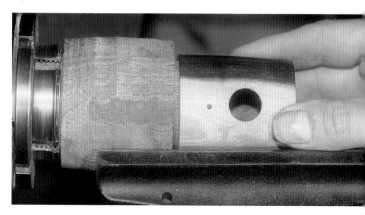

Figure 250. Test fit the tenon. It must not be tight or it will break the thin wall of the house body.

Use your bowl gouge to cut the bottom shape of the floor. (See Figure 251.) Lightly sand the bottom of the house. (See Figure 252.)

Figure 251. Shape the body of the floor with a small bowl gouge.

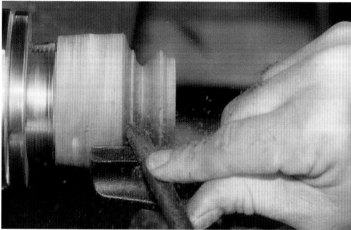

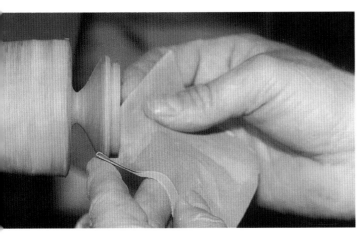

Figure 252. Sand the floor before you part it off.

Part the floor off using your thin parting tool. Now mount the floor into your 4-jaw chuck. Do not squeeze hard with the 4-jaw chuck. A light grip is all that you need. Notice the hole in the center of the floor in Figure 253. This was a pre-existing hole, which determined the size of the tenons that went into the roof and floor. Shape the floor with either your skew or bowl gouge. Sand and apply finish.

Figure 253. Reverse the floor and mount the tenon into the 4-jaw chuck. Be gentle when tightening the jaws. Refine the shape of the floor. Notice the pre-existing hole in the floor. This determined the tenon size that went into the floor and roof.

Making the Roof

Making the roof is identical to making the floor. Use your calipers to measure the inside thickness of the roof. Make a short tenon this size. Test to make sure the fit is just right. Not too tight nor too lose. (See Figure 254.) In this photograph the floor is resting in the house. No glue has been applied. The length of the tenon is about 1/8 of an inch long. (See Figure 255.) Create a cone shaped roof by removing wood toward the headstock. (See Figure 255.)

Figure 254. Make another tenon to fit the roof of the house. Test fit of the roof and bottom at the same time.

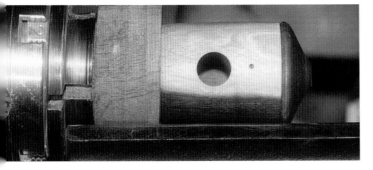

Figure 255. Start shaping the roof with a small bowl gouge.

Reverse the roof on the 4-jaw chuck. Gently grab the 1/8-inch long tenon with the 4-jaw chuck. (See Figure 256.) Gently shape the roof with a bowl gouge or skew. (See Figure 256.) The narrowness of my roof was determined by a preexisting hole in my turning block. Sand and apply finish. I used wax for this project. (See Figure 257.) Check to make sure that the roof and floor fit well. (See Figure 258.)

Figure 256. Reverse the roof and put the tenon into the 4-jaw chuck. This will allow you to cut the very end of the roof.

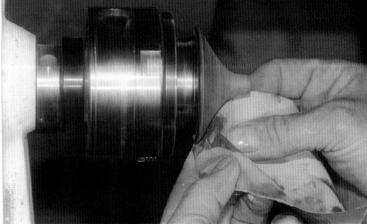

Figure 257. Sand the roof and apply finish.

Figure 258. Test fit the floor and roof.

Speed for Small Turnings

You finally get to adjust the speed of your lathe to a higher speed. For very small turnings like the finial a higher speed is desirable. The high speed will allow you to get a smoother cut. Set your speed to about 1200 RPM.

Making the Roof Finial

Place a new piece of wood in your 4-jaw chuck. Use you skew to cut a small "Jeanie Bottle." Then use you skew to cut a small tenon beneath the "Jeanie Bottle." (See Figure 259.) Make sure that your skew is very sharp. Use your calipers to get the correct diameter. Sand and apply finish. (See Figure 260.) Use your thin parting tool to cut the finial off.

Figure 259. Use your 1/2-inch skew to make the little finial for the roof. Use your calipers to make the tenon the correct size.

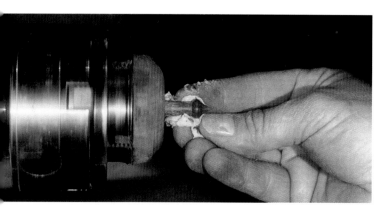

Figure 260. Sand and apply finish to the roof finial.

Making the Perch

The perch is 1/16 of an inch in diameter. This is small!! But you can turn something that small if you follow a few rules. First, use good wood. Soft wood like pine will not stay together. Second, set the lathe speed at a higher speed. I set my speed up to approximately 1800 RPM. Third, your skew must be razor sharp. Fourth, cut very slowly and gently.

Make a little ball on the end of the perch. This is just for bragging rights. Then slowly reduce the tenon to the proper diameter. (See Figure 261.) Sand only with 400 grit sandpaper. Do this very gently. Apply wax with your fingers and use a small piece of tissue paper to buff.

Figure 261. Use your skew to cut a small perch. Make a little ball on the end of the perch.

Making the Floor Finial

The floor finial is made in the same way as the roof finial. Place a new piece of wood in your 4-jaw chuck. Use you skew to cut a small "Acorn." Start by cutting a tenon that is the diameter of the widest part of the acorn. Make a step for the bottom half of the acorn. Then use your skew to taper the end of the acorn. (See Figure 262.) Next, round the corner of the acorn lid as it goes into the bottom. Then taper the cap of the acorn to a point. (See Figure 263.)

Figure 262. Use a 1/2-inch skew to make an acorn finial for the floor.

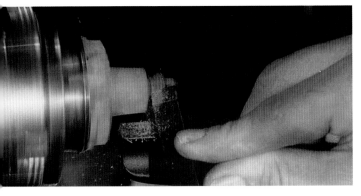

Figure 263. Round over the top of the acorn with your 1/2-inch round skew.

Use your skew to cut a small bead above the acorn and then a larger half bead above that. This half bead will cover the hole where the tenon goes into the floor. (See Figures 264-265.)

Use your calipers to measure the correct thickness of the tenon. (See Figure 265.) Part off with your parting tool.

Figure 264. Cut the tenon with your 1/2-inch round skew.

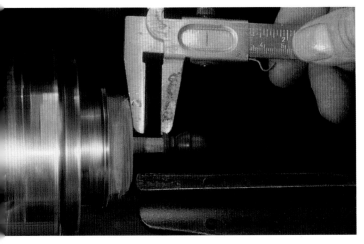

Figure 265. Use your calipers to make sure the diameter is correct.

Assembling the House

Use a small amount of cyano-acrylic glue to assemble the birdhouse. It is easy to make a mess with cyano-acrylic glue, so it might be a good idea to put a small amount of cyano-acrylic glue into a coke bottle lid and apply the glue with a small cotton swab. (See Figure 266.)

Figure 266. Use cyano-acrylic glue to glue the parts together. Be careful not to make a mess.

Displaying the Bird House

You can easily make a display stand using a piece of scrap wood. The base is a simple turning. The support rod is a piece of brass welding rod. I drilled a small hole through the roof finial. I threaded a piece of black thread through the hole and tied it in a loop. This was hooked over the brass hook.

Conclusion

Congratulations!! You have just completed a difficult turning and in the process created a small piece of art!!! Do not be surprised if you have to make several attempts to make some of your parts. This is a difficult project. But it is worth the effort. You are creating something very pretty and in the process you are developing a lot of turning skills.

Figure 267. The finished bird house with homemade stand.

Gallery

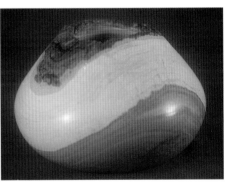

Gallery Contributors

I would like to thank professional turners: Kelly Dunn, Max Krimmel, Robert Rosand, and Phil Brennion for providing photographs of their turnings for this gallery. The work of masters like these can inspire you to improve your own work. To see terrific work from other masters, you may go to my web site at http://www.woodturningplus.com.

1. Kelly Dunn is a professional wood lathe artist who lives on the north end of the big island of Hawaii. Kelly specializes in woods grown on the big island. He creates bowls, hollow vessels, and art forms full time for art galleries and private collectors. Kelly may be contacted at http://jkellydunn.com/

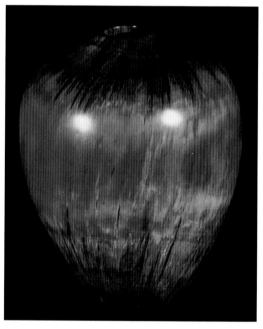

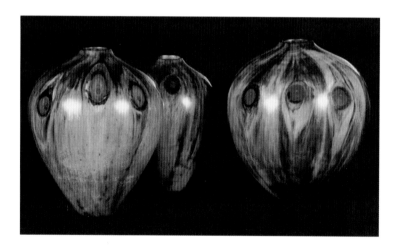

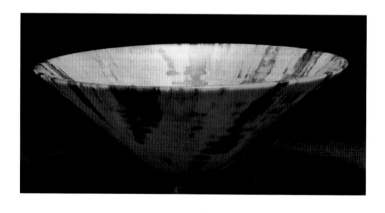

2. Max Krimmel, of Colorado, does some of the most beautiful alabaster turnings in the world. His turnings are more translucent than any others that I have seen. Max is a talented turning artist, musician, and guitar maker. He also does float trips. You can contact Max at: 15 Sherwood Road, Nederland, CO 80466, (303) 258-7723, or http://www.maxkrimmel.com/index.html.

3. Robert Rosand is a professional turner from Bloomsburg, Pennsylvania. He is a member of the AAW and is on his second term as a member of the Board of Directors of the AAW. Bob specializes in small beautiful turnings. He is a frequent contributor to *American Woodturner*. Robert may be contacted at: RROSAND@ptdrolog.net, 570-784-6158.

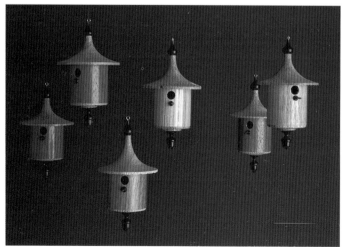